Family History on the Move

Acknowledgements

The authors would like to thank the following:
Mark Hawkins-Dady and Catherine Bradley, who
commissioned and oversaw the book for the
National Archives; Liz Jones (copy editor);
Rosie Anderson (proofreader); and
Zeb Korycinska (indexer).

Family History on the Move

Where your ancestors went and why

Roger Kershaw and Mark Pearsall

the national archives

First published in 2006 by
The National Archives
Kew, Richmond
Surrey, TW9 4DU, UK

www.nationalarchives.gov.uk

The National Archives (TNA) was formed when the Public Record
Office (PRO) and Historical Manuscripts Commission (HMC) combined in
April 2003.

© Roger Kershaw and Mark Pearsall 2006

The right of Roger Kershaw and Mark Pearsall to be identified as
the Authors of this Work has been asserted by them in accordance with
the Copyright, Designs and Patents Act 1988.

All rights reserved. No part of this publication may be reproduced,
stored in a retrieval system or transmitted, in any form or by any
means, electronic, mechanical, photocopying, recording or otherwise
without the prior permission of both the copyright holder and the
above publisher.

A catalogue card for this book is available from the British Library.

ISBN 1 903365 92 9
978 1 903365 80 9

Typeset by Gem Graphics, Trenance, Cornwall
Cover designed by Penny Jones and Michael Morris
Printed by MPG Books, Bodmin, Cornwall

Contents

Picture acknowledgements

Front cover. Jessie McEwan and Tilda Monaghan aboard the Orient Line *Ormonde* (1947), which carried emigrants from London to Sydney. The passenger list is at the National Archives (BT 27/1607). Image © Hulton-Deutsch Collection/CORBIS

Back cover. A family group on board the *Marlock* (c.1920s), en route from the Hebrides to a new life in Canada. Image © Hulton-Deutsch Collection/CORBIS.

p. 4 The 'List of Aliens' provided by the master of the *Sir Edward Banks* on arrival at the port of London, 19 November 1842, showing Friedrich Engels as one of his passengers (the eighth name on the list) (TNA HO 3/26).

p. 20 Passengers on the SS *Empire Windrush* (1948), berthed at Tilbury, London, having sailed from the Caribbean. Image courtesy of Topfoto.co.uk (N19136a).

p. 42 The naturalization certificate for Ernst Freud and his family (1939) (TNA HO 334/228 (BZ 1216)).

p. 64 A group of Belgian refugees in Britain during the First World War, employed in shell manufacture. Image by kind permission of the Imperial War Museum, London (Q27740).

p. 90 Children of aliens interned during the Second World War, performing exercises on the beach, Isle of Man (TNA HO 213/1053).

p. 118 'Monarchs of the Sea' poster (1907), advertising the Cunard Line ships *Lusitania* and *Mauretania* (TNA COPY 1/259/ii).

p. 142 'A Note of the Ship' (1619), recording the ships, men and provisions being sent to Virginia (TNA CO 1/1/155).

p. 160 Advertisement (1834) by the British government's Emigration Committee promoting female passage to Van Diemen's Land (Tasmania) (TNA CO 384/35/10).

p. 182 A game of cricket (1902) on the deck of the SS *Runic* en route to Cape Town, South Africa (TNA COPY 1/455).

p. 204 A notice (1884) from the 'Guardians of the Poor of the Poplar Union', London, announcing the names of abandoned children being considered for emigration to Canada (TNA MH12/7698).

p. 224 A burial at sea (1884), on an ocean-going passenger steamship (TNA COPY 1/369).

Introduction: why migrate?

In 2005 the number of immigrants arriving in the United Kingdom outstripped those emigrating by a larger margin than at any time previously. Britain has often been described as a nation of immigrants: the Flemish in the 1500s, Huguenots in the late 1600s, the Irish in the 1700s and 1800s, a Jewish influx in the late 1800s, and migrants from the colonies and Poland after the Second World War, as well as more recently migrants from the European Union. However, during the same period, probably 17 million people left the British Isles.

The outward and inward flux of people across the centuries remains a subject of wide fascination, as witnessed by the second series (2006) of the television programme *Who Do You Think You Are?*, in which five of the six episodes examined ancestors who were, at some point, on the move.

The Industrial Revolution accelerated the movement of population from the countryside to the expanding towns of Georgian and Victorian

Britain. The workforce needed to supply the new factories and service industries, while the decline of the rural economy also saw the movement of people from Wales, Scotland and Ireland into England. Many Irish and some Scots also moved between Ireland and Scotland. (To trace domestic movements, the core records are often the same as for one's sedentary ancestors: census and parish records, wills, non-conformist registers, Poor Law records, and so forth: see the National Archives website for an introduction to these.)

The search for a better life within national borders was not, of course, always a success. Under the 17th-century Settlement Acts, people moving around Britain in search of work needed a settlement certificate, a kind of internal passport. This confirmed their legal parish of settlement (often where they were born), to which they would have to return should they become destitute. For the 19th century, Poor Law records (now at county records offices and the National Archives of England and of Scotland) reveal the names of those who needed help (or who failed to get it). The category included those admitted to workhouses and itinerant/seasonal labourers, such as those who flooded across the Irish Sea following the Great Famine.

Across borders, the decision to migrate has often been voluntary, albeit for pressing or seemingly unavoidable reasons: to seek political or religious freedom, to escape war, or to take a gamble on lifting oneself and one's family out of destitution as so many Irish did in the aftermath of the 19th century's Great Famine. Involuntary, enforced migration relates mainly to transportation – that practice of exiling convicts overseas to the New World, during which time they would be made to work productively and learn new habits of industry. There is also the vexed issue of child migration, which could hardly be described as a voluntary enterprise on the part of the child.

This book examines the reasons behind the movement of people and identifies key sources for family historians. (Some parts of the book have appeared in an earlier version, in *Immigrants and Aliens*, 2004 and *Emigrants and Expats*, 2002.) It also attempts to identify pitfalls and provide useful research tips. It is impossible to cover everything, but the book does not restrict itself to the resources of the National Archives, immensely rich though these are. Records of migrants are as scattered across the globe as the migrants themselves, and *Family History on the Move* seeks to represent that spread.

Roger Kershaw and Mark Pearsall

A LIST OF ALIENS.

I, the undersigned, being Master of the *Sir Edw Banks*

bound from *Ostend* to the Port of London

do, in compliance with the Provisions of an Act of Parliament, passed in the 6th William IV. Cap. 11, hereby declare, that the following is a full and true Account, to the best of my knowledge, of all Aliens who are now on board my said Ship or Vessel, or have landed herefrom in this Realm, with their Names, Rank, Occupation and Description.

Broker's Name *Breadhead Spicer*   Master's Name *J Robinson*

No.	Christian and Surnames. Prenoms et Noms.	Quality. Profession.	Country Pays
	M Edersheim	Particulier	Holland
	Fanny his Wife & Daughter	—	Vienna
	J. W. Finck	Courier	Prussian
	Ths van Kempette	particulier	Belgique
	P J Kayser	Fabribant	Frankfort
	Siman Hoppen	Particulier	München Bayon
	H Fries	Negociant	
	Fredk Engels	Merchant	Prussia
	A Erbslöh		
	Ph H. Reinhard	Merchand	Mannheim (Rhein)
	Charles Bonns	Domestic	London

To the Chief Officer of the Customs at the Port of *London*

Dated this   day of *18 Nov*

1842

Records of arrival

Tracking down an ancestor who immigrated to the United Kingdom after about 1890 is considerably easier than tracing an earlier arrival. In the earlier period, it is difficult – and unfortunately in many cases impossible – to discover when an ancestor first arrived.

Many records that once existed have not survived. Where records do survive there are gaps and omissions, and the regulations under the Aliens Acts in the early 19th century were sometimes flouted. Unless your ancestor applied for the rights and obligations that came with 'denization' or 'naturalization' (see Chapter 3 for elaboration of these concepts), and the majority did not, you may not be able to pin down a year of arrival, let alone a specific date. You may have to fall back on the 10-yearly census returns from 1841 as well as baptismal and birth records of children to provide clues for an approximate period of arrival.

Restrictions and records, 18th–19th centuries

Surviving records of actual arrival are rare before the 19th century. The systematic recording of aliens coming into the country was introduced by an Act of 1793. This Act was renewed frequently, and subsequent Acts in

1816, 1826 and 1836 regulated the system. A superintendent of aliens was appointed after the Act of 1793 and an Aliens Office was created, which came directly under the control of the Home Office from 1836.

Aliens arriving in Britain had to be recorded on entry at the ports and registered with the local Justices of the Peace and their details forwarded to the Aliens Office in London. As well as having to register with the magistrate, if they wished to move from their port of arrival they had to obtain permission and be issued with a 'passport' for travelling to and from each place in the kingdom. A very small number of lists of aliens arriving at British ports survive among Foreign Office records for the brief period from August 1810 to May 1811.

However, most of the early records were later destroyed, leaving only some indexes from 1826 to 1849 and certificates of arrival from 1836 to 1852. Even for those periods where certificates of arrival and passenger lists survive, there was evasion and neglect in enforcing the Acts, where masters did not provide lists and aliens did not register, so the surviving documentation is far from a complete record of aliens entering the country.

Licences and regulations, 18th–19th centuries

To actually reside in the country immigrants had to obtain a licence from the Aliens Office. These licences had to be shown to the householders with whom they were to lodge or reside and the householder had to inform the parish constable or a local Justice of the Peace. They also had to inform the parish overseers of the poor. 'Accounts of Aliens' and 'Householders' Notices' and 'Overseers' Returns' were sent to the Clerk of the Peace so that he could lay them before the Justices of the Peace at the Quarter Sessions. No details of licences issued by the Aliens Office unfortunately survive in the National Archives. However, some records of registration, including examples of licences, or details of them can survive among Quarter Sessions records held locally in county record offices.

The Napoleonic wartime regulations regarding aliens were repealed at the peace of 1814, but were subsequently renewed later in that same year and again in 1815. In 1816 a further Aliens Act was passed. It required masters of vessels to declare in writing to the Inspector of Aliens or an officer of the Customs the number of aliens on board his ship, specifying their names and descriptions, and the aliens themselves were required to make a similar declaration. Each alien was to be issued on arrival with a certificate, showing the ship's name, and his or her own name, description, place of departure, destination and profession, with space for references and remarks. Unless they were a servant, the alien was to produce the certificate within one week to a magistrate or Justice of the Peace, and copies of the details on the certificates were to be sent both by the port and by the magistrate to the Secretary of State in London. The Act applied to all aliens except foreign seamen, ambassadors and their domestic servants, and children under 14. Most of these provisions had previously been included in the 1793 Act but the new Act made the first provision for any central system of registration. It was, however, confined to aliens arriving in the country from 1816 and did not apply to those who had arrived previously.

The Aliens Acts from 1826

The Aliens Act 1826 required that from 1 July 1826 every alien should make a declaration 'of his name, abode, etc.' and transmit the same within 14 days to the Aliens Office in Great Britain, or in Ireland to the Chief Secretary. Aliens were thereafter required to send to the Secretary of State, or to the Chief Secretary for Ireland, a declaration of their place of residence every six months, and the clerk at the Aliens Office was to send in return a certificate similar to that described in the 1816 Act. The requirements of the 1793 and 1816 Acts regarding the declaration to be made by masters of vessels and by aliens on arrival were retained, together with the requirement that aliens arriving in this country should be given certificates and copies sent to the Secretary of State. Aliens were no longer required to produce their certificates to a magistrate or Justice of the Peace, but they were to produce them at the Aliens Office if residing within five miles of the City of Westminster, or to make a declaration in writing if they lived further away. They were also required to make a declaration to the Aliens Office should they wish to leave the country.

As with the 1816 Act, this Act did not apply to foreign seamen, ambassadors or their domestic ser-vants, or children under 14, and a new provision was included to the effect that aliens should also be exempt who had been continually residing in the country for at least seven years, provided they held a certificate to this effect from the Aliens Office. This Act remained in force until 1836.

Another Act was passed in 1836 and this

repealed the Act of 1826; it introduced some relaxation in the system of registration but continued the requirement that masters of vessels and aliens should make a declaration on arrival. Aliens were still given a certificate, and copies of the certificates were sent to the Secretary of State in London. Aliens were still required to produce registration certificates but it was no longer necessary for them to visit or send a written declaration to the Aliens Office, and the declaration they made on leaving the country was in future to be made at the Customs Office at the port of departure. An alien living in this country was no longer required to report his or her address every six months, and was in future to become exempt from the provisions of the Act after three years instead of seven.

This Act remained in force until it was repealed by the Aliens Act 1905. The provisions of the 1816, 1826 and 1836 Acts were directed mainly against foreign 'criminal and hostile persons' and they were concerned with maintaining a check on aliens entering or already in the country rather than with excluding them from entry altogether. It was not until the end of the 19th century that any concern was felt at the likely effect of alien immigration on the employment situation of British workers, and it was not until 1905 that any provision was made to deal with such immigration.

The preservation of passenger lists

The Merchant Shipping Acts required the keeping of ships' passenger lists for British registered vessels. The lists were deposited by the master or shipping company with the Board of Trade. Early lists no longer survive but some arrival lists survive from 1878 to 1888, and the majority from 1890 to 1960. They contain the names of people arriving in the country and give age, occupation and (from 1922) the intended address in the United Kingdom of each passenger. There is no indication as to how long people intended to stay but from the 1930s entries include the abbreviation 'T' if the visit was for the purpose of tourism. There are separate lists for British (and Commonwealth) passengers and alien passengers. If a vessel called into a European port before arriving in Britain then there will be lists of passengers who boarded the ship for the final leg of the voyage. Unfortunately no lists survive for cross-channel packet boats (delivering mail) or ferries, or for any ship commencing its voyage from continental Europe.

Spotlight: Karl Marx and Friedrich Engels

The theorists of communism Karl Marx (1818–83) and Friedrich Engels (1820–95) both migrated to England in the 1840s, but only one of them received an alien's certificate of arrival.

According to his biographies, Marx first visited London and Manchester in the Summer of 1845 before being expelled from Prussia and moving permanently to London in August 1849. At the National Archives, no certificate of arrival survives for Marx in series HO 2 for any of these visits. However, his name is recorded on a list of alien passengers in HO 3/53 arriving in London on 27 August 1849, aboard the *City of Bologne* from Bologne. He is listed as 'Dr Charles Marx'. His wife Jenny appears in the same document, arriving on 19 September 1849, on the *Albion*, again travelling from Bologne to London.

Engels, meanwhile, came from Prussia to England in November 1842 to work in his father's Manchester textile firm, Ermen and Engels. He was issued with a certificate, which can be found at HO 2/1089 (4270), that shows he entered the port of London on 19 November 1842 on the vessel *Sir Edward Banks*. His name also appears in the list of alien passengers in HO 3/26 (see illustration on p. 4).

After 1960 passenger lists have not been permanently preserved and transferred to the National Archives. With the growth of airline companies and travel by air, it was decided not to keep later ships' passenger lists after their administrative life was over. Aircraft passenger lists have never been permanently preserved either, and are only kept for the duration of their administrative life.

Discovering the records

Lists of aliens and certificates of arrival
Lists of aliens arriving at British ports between August 1810 and May 1811 are held in the National Archives (TNA) in the Foreign Office series FO 83/21–22.

Certificates of arrival only survive from 1836 to 1852 in the National Archives Home Office series HO 2, although there are indexes from 1826 to 1849 in HO 5/25–32. Earlier certificates were destroyed in 1836. The certificates from 1836 are arranged under port of arrival and each certificate gives the individual's nationality, profession, date of arrival and last country visited (not necessarily their country of origin) and their signature. Separate accounts of aliens arriving in the port of London between July and November

1826 can be found in CUST 102/393–395. Similarly, CUST 102/396 includes accounts of aliens arriving in the port of Gravesend between October 1826 and August 1837.

There is an unpublished index to some German, Prussian and Polish arrivals between 1847 and 1852, compiled by the Anglo-German Family History Society, a copy of which is available in the Research Enquiries Room at the National Archives.

Returns of alien passengers made by masters of ships under section 2 of the Aliens Act 1836 are in TNA series HO 3. They consist of lists of names of alien passengers with no other personal details. These returns only survive up to 1859.

Some entry books of correspondence and out-letters of the Aliens Office from 1794 can be found in TNA series HO 5.

The London Metropolitan Archives holds in the Middlesex Quarter Sessions records of 38 accounts of aliens from eight parishes in Middlesex in 1797, and 10 householders' notices from five Middlesex parishes in 1798. Other county record offices Quarter Sessions records should be searched for similar returns of aliens. You can consult the Access to Archives website for details of holdings.

Passenger lists

The Merchant Shipping Act 1894 (57 & 58 Victoria, c. 60) required the listing of passengers on board British merchant vessels. Ships' passenger lists among the records of the Board of Trade relate mainly to arrivals in and departures from UK seaports, including Ireland before 1924. The lists were deposited with the Board of Trade by the various passenger shipping lines.

Passenger lists of inward voyages to the United Kingdom from destinations outside Europe and the Mediterranean Sea survive from 1878 to 1888 and from 1890 to 1960 in the National Archives, in the Board of Trade series BT 26. Many lists earlier than 1890 were destroyed by order of the Board in 1900, but a few accidentally escaped destruction and are included in this series. They are arranged in date order by the port of arrival. Unfortunately they are not indexed by name of passenger, so unless you know the port of arrival and ship, and an approximate date, a speculative search would be too time-consuming to undertake. However, there is an on-going catalogue improvement project, called Travel to the UK, to improve information online; in addition to port and date of arrival, this provides the names of the ship, shipping companies and original port of departure. The project will eventually make the series BT 32 redundant. BT 32, available on the open shelves in the research enquiries room at the National Archives at Kew, consists of registers of passenger lists kept by the Board of Trade's Commercial, Labour and Statistical Department and its successors. Before 1920 they give, under the different ports, the names of ships and the month of arrival and departure; after 1920 the date of arrival or departure is recorded. Before 1908 the registers relate only to the ports of Southampton, Bristol and Weymouth. They are useful in identifying passenger lists if a name of a ship is known but the port of arrival or departure is not known.

The inward lists in TNA series BT 26 provide details of all passengers arriving at UK ports, Passenger lists for ships whose voyages began within Europe are not included. The information available from these lists varies, but can include age, address in UK (from 1922) and occupation. Lists after the 1930s indicate whether or not passengers were travelling for tourist/ leisure reasons by using the abbreviation 'T'. There are also separate lists for British and alien passengers.

In addition to the records described above, TNA series ADM 30/35 contains passenger lists of HM steam packets carrying passengers to,

from and within the Mediterranean area 1831 to
1834.

The Moving Here website contains digitized
images (free to search and download) of inwards
passenger lists from March 1948 to October 1960
which brought groups of Indian and Caribbean migrants to the UK – these lists have been
indexed by name of ship and by name of person.

An overseas source
The Hamburg State Archive in Germany holds
lists of passengers sailing from the port of
Hamburg to overseas destinations directly and
indirectly, including the United Kingdom (*see also*
Chapter 7). These surviving lists cover the period
from 1850 to 1934, with a break from 1914 to
1920 because of the First World War. The Latter-
day Saints (Mormon) Family History Library has
copies of these lists on microfilm which can be
ordered and seen in their family history centres.
The direct and indirect lists for 1850–5 are
arranged alphabetically by the first letter of the
surname of the head of household. There are
separate indexes for the direct and indirect
lists from 1855 to 1910, and then a single index
for both series from 1911. The indexes for
1855–1914 are arranged by the first letter of the
surname of the head of the household, and then

chronologically by the date the vessels sailed from Hamburg. The indexes for 1920–34 are in strict alphabetical order. A card index to the direct lists for the period 1850–71 and to the indirect lists for the years 1854–67 is held in the Hamburg State Archive, which will search this index for a fee. The Latter-day Saints Family History Library has a copy of this index on 46 microfilm reels.

Chapter 2

Settling into the community

- The Jewish community
- Early Afro-Caribbean settlement
- Colonial immigration
- South Asian immigration
- Discovering the records
  The 'Moving Here' website
  Jewish records
  The black community
  Asian communities
  Lists of colonial immigrants
  Immigration vouchers
  Immigration administration and police files

After arrival immigrants faced the task of settling into the community. Sometimes people did this quickly, assimilating either by choice or – in some cases – necessity; others, settling in an area of fellow immigrants based usually on a common language or religion, or both, retained a separate identity for longer periods. You will have seen that aliens' legislation after 1793 required magistrates to keep a check on their movements and places of settlement. Many records have not survived, but it is worth checking Quarter Sessions records and parish records for the places your ancestors settled. Parish records, in particular records of the churchwardens, constables and Overseers of the Poor, and after 1834 records of the Poor Law Unions, are worth examining. Records of charities and charitable institutions, where they survive, can be a useful source to trace new arrivals settling into a community. For 19th-century arrivals the census returns from 1841 to 1901 should be searched, which you can now do online.

The Jewish community

The Jewish community was expelled from England by Edward I in 1290 and it was not until 1656 that Jews were legally permitted to settle again in England. However, some Jews nominally accepting the Christian faith did live in England before this, following the expulsion of the Jews from Spain in 1492. A small group of Portuguese Jews also settled in London during the reign of Elizabeth I. Their commercial connections and hatred of Spain made many of these 'Marranos' useful to the English government and the Elizabethan intelligence service. Legal resettlement, however, came after the Civil War, during the Commonwealth period, when Oliver Cromwell permitted Jews to resettle in England. The Council of State heard their petition and in November 1655 resolved 'that the Jews deserving it may be admitted into this nation to trade and traffic and dwell amongst us as Providence shall give occasion'. The petition and a humble address were referred to a committee for consideration. The petition asked that the Jews might be allowed to live in England, have synagogues and cemeteries, and trade freely. The lawyers quickly decided that there was no legal bar to re-admission and the committee made a favourable report, although they laid down several conditions.

The legal position of the Marranos was brought to a head in 1656 when they again petitioned for permission for Jews to meet for worship in their houses and to bury their dead outside the City of London. No reply or order of the Council of State appears to have survived, but from this time on Jews were permitted to live and worship in England. In December 1656 they rented land in Creechurch Lane, London, for a synagogue and later bought land for a cemetery. Immigrants arriving from the 1650s onward were Sephardi Jews (Portuguese, Spanish and Italian) from southern Europe. Later, during the 1680s, Ashkenazi Jews from central and eastern Europe began to arrive in the 1680s from Holland and Bohemia (the main influx of Ashkenazim from Russia and Poland was not until the end of the 19th century). By about 1690 there were enough German Jews for a separate Ashkenazi community in London. Their first synagogue, the Great Synagogue, was opened in 1722.

Early Afro-Caribbean settlement

Afro-Caribbean settlement in Britain began to develop in the ports of London, Bristol and the south coast in the 16th century as a result of voyages to Africa and the development of the slave trade. Such was the increase of Africans in England that in 1596 Elizabeth I ordered that they should be expelled, and in 1601 a proclamation was issued stating that 'the great number of Negroes and Blackamoors which (as she is informed) are crept into this realm' should be 'with all speed avoided and discharged out of this her majesty's dominions'. Such measures, however, made very little difference over time and the numbers of Africans continued to grow in the 17th and 18th centuries. A free community grew up in the ports of London, Liverpool and Bristol, where Afro-Caribbean sailors, former slaves and their families lived. The aristocracy, gentry and merchants brought back slaves from their plantations to become domestic servants. These in turn would gain their freedom, or they might run away and lose themselves in London or the large towns and ports.

It is not always easy to trace Afro-Caribbeans among the records as you are normally dependent on them being described as such. You can often find such entries referring to people of colour in parish registers, in particular baptisms and burials of servants. Before 1813 and the introduction of pro forma registers, clergymen would often add comments on parishioners or descriptions of them. Wills of the aristocracy, gentry and merchant classes can provide information on servants and former slaves. Francis Barber appears in the will of his master, Colonel Richard

Bathurst of the Close, Lincoln, in 1756, where he was bequeathed his freedom and a legacy of £12. Barber then went on to become servant to no less a man than the lexicographer and wit Samuel Johnson: a free man in domestic service, not a slave. He later became the chief beneficiary under Johnson's will.

Many Afro-Caribbean men who were not slaves or domestic servants were seamen in the Merchant Navy and the Royal Navy. Ships' musters of merchant vessels from 1747 and agreements and crew lists from 1835 may therefore be worth consulting. Registration of merchant seamen began in 1835 with three series of registers of seamen and a register of seamen's tickets to 1857. Later registration records, the fourth and fifth registry from 1913 to 1972, can be used to trace merchant seamen in the 20th century.

Colonial immigration

As a result of the Second World War, many colonial subjects were recruited for war service in the United Kingdom and many stayed after the war. A postwar labour shortage led the government to encourage recruitment of workers from the colonies and also from Ireland. The British government created a Ministry of Labour working party in 1948 to look into the problem of unemployment in the colonies, particularly the West Indies. The committee was concerned about the discrimination that black workers would face coming to Britain and the difficulties involved in assimilating them. It therefore recommended no large-scale immigration of male colonial workers; instead it favoured the recruitment of female workers, noting the serious labour shortages in domestic employment, the Health Service and textile industries. However, as they were British subjects, people from the colonies were not restricted from coming to the UK to find employment. It was the Commonwealth Immigrants Act 1962 that eventually put an end to easy immigration from the Commonwealth.

This Act was the culmination of mounting public pressure for some restriction on immigration from the colonies. The fear of control, however, brought in larger numbers of migrants from the Caribbean in 1961 and 1962. The Act required all Commonwealth citizens seeking employment in Britain to qualify for a voucher, and laid special emphasis on controlling unskilled workers. And people with passports not issued in Britain were obliged to hold a work permit to secure their entry. The later Commonwealth

Spotlight: Floella Benjamin

The arrival of the SS Empire Windrush (see illustration on p. 20) at Tilbury docks, London, on 22 June 1948 heralded the start of colonial migration to the UK after the Second World War. The ship travelled from Jamaica carrying 492 passengers wishing to start new lives. In the years following, some 160,000 West Indians migrated to the UK. One was Floella Benjamin, who was born in Trinidad in 1949 and migrated with her family to the UK in 1960. She became well known as a successful presenter on children's television in the 1980s and was awarded the OBE (Order of the British Empire) in 2000 for services to broadcasting.

Her arrival record at the National Archives (BT 26/1460) can be downloaded free from the Moving Here website. Her name is included on the list of the *Marques de Comillas*, travelling from the West Indies to Southampton in September 1960. Eleven-year old Floella travelled with her siblings Sandra (12), Lester (9) and Ellington (7) and, on arrival, settled in Chiswick, West London.

Immigrants Act 1968 further tightened controls, potential immigrants now being required to prove that they had been born in the United Kingdom or that their parents or grandparents had been.

The issuing of vouchers was ended by the Immigration Act 1971, which came into force on 1 January 1973. This Act brought Commonwealth citizens into line with citizens of other countries, in so far as employment was concerned, which meant that Commonwealth citizens had to have a prospective employer in order to come to this country to work.

South Asian immigration

The majority of migrants from the Indian sub-continent arrived in Britain in the 1950s and 1960s. We would suggest you contact the social and cultural organizations of the particular South Asian communities in which you are interested to explore their history further. It is also worth consulting the Caribbean Studies Black and Asian History website and the Moving Here website and database.

South Asians with British passports who were expelled from Kenya settled in the UK in 1967, as did South Asians expelled from Uganda in 1973. The Uganda Resettlement Board was appointed by the Home Secretary to assist UK passport-holders and their dependents. Their reception in the UK was undertaken with the help of voluntary organizations and local authorities.

Temporary accommodation was provided, mainly in resettlement centres, and people were discouraged from going to areas where services were particularly under stress and where houses were unlikely to be available.

Discovering the records

The 'Moving Here' website
Moving Here (*www.movinghere.org.uk*) is a website showing why people came to England over the last 200 years and what their experiences have been and continue to be. It gives free access, for personal and educational use, to an online catalogue of original material related to migration history from local, regional and national archives, libraries and museums. It provides a wealth of information relating to the migration of Caribbean, Irish, Jewish and South Asian communities to England over the last two hundred years. The site also includes sound recordings and video clips, and individuals can contribute their own stories and experiences to the site.

Jewish records
Synagogues themselves usually hold genealogical records of the Jewish community from the period of resettlement. The London Metropolitan

Archives (LMA) holds records of a number of organizations of local, national and international significance, but very few genealogical records. The Bevis Marks Hall has a collection of Jewish registers from 1687 to 1837. The records of the Board of Deputies of British Jews, the representative body of British Jewry, are held in the London Metropolitan Archives (LMA ref. ACC/3121) but are only available with the permission of the Board of Deputies. The Board was founded in 1760 as the London Committee of Deputies of British Jews, when representatives of the Sephardi and Ashkenazi communities in London met and presented a loyal address to George III on his accession to the throne.

Other Jewish records are also held elsewhere. Most of the refugees settled in or around London and the records of the Jewish Temporary Shelter are available at the London Metropolitan Archives. Personal files of approximately 400,000 Jewish refugees are still kept by the Jewish Refugees Committee. Further information on Jewish immigrants is available at the Hartley Library, University of Southampton, and at the Manchester Local Studies Unit, but access to these archives may be restricted.

The Chief Rabbi's Office hold case files of adoptions, conversions, divorces and also certificates of evidence for much of the 19th and 20th centuries. With the exception of the certificates of evidence, all other documents are confidential and information will only be sent to those with a legitimate legal interest. The certificates of evidence were required by the Chief Rabbi to authorize marriages, and they contain details of the applicant's date, age and place of birth and/or marriage abroad. The certificates often contain additional information to those issued by the Registrar General's Office and are particularly useful for tracing those who did not naturalize, where information about their origin or marriage abroad may not exist elsewhere. The Chief Rabbi's Office only accepts visits by prior appointment.

PROBATE

The wills proved in the Prerogative Court of Canterbury (PROB) from 1384 to 1858 can be searched for through the National Archives website. Probate records of the Prerogative Court of Canterbury include wills, administrations and related documents of prominent Jewish families, and extracts have been published by the Jewish Genealogical Society of Great Britain.

Additional information about the estates of leading Jews for the 18th and 19th centuries may be found in the National Archives series IR 26: Estate Duty Office: Registers of Legacy Duty, Succession Duty and Estate Duty.

PRIVY COUNCIL AND STATE PAPER RECORDS

In the National Archives series PC 2: Privy Council Registers and State Papers Domestic, you should consult *Acts of the Privy Council* and the *Calendars of State Papers, Domestic* for references to the 17th- and 18th-century Jewish community. Copies can be found in the Map and Large Document Room, and in many libraries.

HOME OFFICE AND METROPOLITAN POLICE RECORDS

At the National Archives, HO 45: Home Office: Registered Files includes material on the immigration of German, Polish and Russian Jews, from 1887 to 1905. Aliens' correspondence generally will be found in series HO 1 or in Domestic Correspondence (HO 42, HO 44, HO 45); out-letters on alien matters generally are in Aliens Entry Books (HO 5) from 1794 to 1921, and those on the working of the Aliens Act 1905 are in Aliens Restriction: Entry Books (HO 162) from 1905 to 1921.

Also at the National Archives, MEPO 2: Correspondence and Papers of the Commissioner of the Metropolitan Police contains material on the arrival of Jewish immigrants, the work of Jewish charities and the settlement of immigrant Jews in the East End of London from 1887 to 1905.

MEPO 35: Aliens Registration Office: Sample Record Cards contains the surviving aliens' registration cards for the London area. These represent some 1,000 cases out of the tens of thousands of aliens resident in London since 1914. Although a small sample, they do include some notable cases.

The black community

The Institute of Commonwealth Studies and the National Archives have created the Caribbean Studies Black and Asian History (CASBAH) website for research resources relating to Caribbean studies and the history of black and Asian peoples in the United Kingdom. The database contains information from a number of archives, with printed and audiovisual resources held in academic, public and specialist libraries and other institutions.

Estate papers of families connected with the slave trade and the West Indies should be searched for records of black servants and slaves. To do this, use the National Register of Archives database and also Access to Archives to locate papers of families who owned estates and plantations.

Probate records are also worth searching for bequests of freedom and legacies to favourite servants. The wills proved in the Prerogative Court of Canterbury from 1384 to 1858 can be searched for online. Wills proved at the Prerogative and Exchequer Courts of York and of 45 peculiar courts from the 14th century to 1858 are at the Borthwick Institute and online at their website. Wills proved in the Bishop's and Archdeacon's Courts and in other probate jurisdictions can be found in the relevant county record offices.

COMMITTEE FOR THE RELIEF OF THE BLACK POOR, 1786
The records of the Committee for the Relief of the Black Poor 1786 are in the National Archives series T 1: Treasury Board Papers (T 1/631–6, 638, 641–7). These include minutes of the Committee (T 1/631–8 and T 1/641) and Henry Smeathman's plan for the settlement of Sierra Leone (T 1/631/1304). For full references to Treasury paper numbers see RISD Memorandum 567 and Domestic Records leaflet 39 at the National Archives.

MERCHANT SEAMEN'S RECORDS

TNA series BT 98: Agreements and Crew Lists, Series I, is arranged by port up to 1854 and then by the ship's official number up to 1860. Unfortunately, only those for Dartmouth, Liverpool, Plymouth and Shields survive before 1800. Only some of the musters include crew names. The agreements and crew lists from 1835 include town or country of birth and other details. Records from 1861 are in BT 99: Agreements and Crew Lists, Series II, but the National Archives hold only a 10 per cent sample for each year; the majority of the others are held by the Maritime History Group, at the Memorial University of Newfoundland.

The National Archives series BT 114: Alphabetical Register of Seamen's Tickets and BT 113: Register of Seamen's Tickets from 1845 to 1854 give places of birth and a physical description of each man. Registration was discontinued after 1857 and only the Agreements and Crew Lists are available until the Central Index Register began in 1913. This is known as the Fourth Register of Seamen and consists of four large card indexes in BT 348–350 and BT 364. The Central Index was replaced by a Central Register of Seamen in 1941, which is sometimes known as the Fifth Register; BT 382: Fifth Register of

Merchant Seamen's Service (CRS 10 forms) covers 1941 to 1972. It is arranged in eight parts covering different ethnic groups. Part One 1941 to 1946 and Part Two 1946 to 1972 cover mainly Europeans but also include men of African and Caribbean descent.

At the National Archives, BT 372: Central Register of Seamen: Seamen's Records ('Pouches') includes records relating to individual seamen filed in a paper envelope 'pouch'. When seamen were discharged, some or all of their documents (including the index cards) were placed in the pouches; these include discharges of some seamen who were originally registered in the Central Index Register of 1913 to 1941. The pouches are arranged by discharge number within a number of series for different Commonwealth countries. They are searchable by name on the National Archives online catalogue.

Asian communities
The British Library Asia, Pacific and Africa Collection has a few references in the India Office Public and Judicial Department annual files (BL references: L/P & J/6 and L/P & J/7) to the provision of assistance made in the 19th and early 20th centuries for destitute Indians in the UK. These people, including seamen and discharged

servants, appear to have become stranded in Britain and needed support. The indexes to these records include names of individuals.

The National Archives series HO 289 consists of files relating to the Uganda Resettlement Board, containing Board meeting, correspondence and other papers. The Board's first meeting was on 30 August 1972, and its final report in April 1974. The first planeload of Ugandan Asians arrived in the UK on 18 September 1972. By the end of the year, some 25,000 had arrived. Other sources relating to this expulsion can be found in records of the Foreign and Commonwealth Office, specifically FCO 31/1375–1401, 1441–1448, FCO 50/396–416, FCO 53/278–280 and FCO 89/9–10 and Department of Education files in ED 269/14 and ED 233/11.

Lists of colonial immigrants
The only lists of colonial immigrants are the inwards passenger lists in BT 26, which survive up to and including 1960. These give the names of all passengers arriving in the UK where the ship's voyage began at a port outside Europe and the Mediterranean Sea. Many passenger lists in BT 26 covering the period 1948–60 have been digitized and indexed by name and are found on the Moving Here website. These are particularly

useful for researching the migration of colonial workers and families by sea for this period.

Many colonial migrants arrived in the UK by plane or by train, entering London Victoria via Calais and Dover after disembarking from ships on the Continent, from such ports as Marseilles, Genoa and Vigo. The National Archives does not hold arrival details for such migrants.

Immigration vouchers
Vouchers for the employment of Commonwealth citizens were issued under the Commonwealth Immigrants Acts 1962 and 1968. The vouchers were issued in two categories: category A for Commonwealth citizens with a definite offer of a job, and category B for those who held certain specified professional qualifications. The prospective employer made application for a category A voucher.

The National Archives series LAB 42 consists of specimen applications. All pieces in this series are open to public inspection following a re-review in 1998.

LAB 48 contains specimen applications from aliens, 1968 to 1972, and, from 1973 onwards, from both aliens and Commonwealth citizens. The majority of these records are open to public inspection following a re-review in 1998.

Immigration administration and police files

Ministry of Labour files relating to employment, welfare and training of colonial migrants can be found at the National Archives in series LAB 8, LAB 13 and LAB 26. These include many papers on Commonwealth migration and labour, including reports and papers on the Commonwealth Immigrants Act 1962.

Metropolitan Police files relating to attitudes towards colonial migrants, the integration of colonial migrants into local communities and issues relating to law and order can be found in TNA series MEPO 2. Cases investigated by the Race Relations Board are in CK 2.

Home Office general files including casework on a variety of immigration and aliens issues can be found in TNA series HO 213, HO 325, HO 352, HO 355, HO 367 and HO 394.

Individual colonies set up schemes and committees to deal with emigration to the UK. Records of such migration schemes can be found in various TNA series, including CO 323: Colonies: General: Original Correspondence and CO 1032: Colonial Office: Defence and General Department and Successors: Registered Files. Correspondence relating to specific colonies may be found under relevant CO (Colonial Office) correspondence series.

DO 35: Dominions Office and Commonwealth Relations Office: Original Correspondence and DO 175: General and Migration Records include files relating to measures for controlling immigration from the colonies during the 1950s. Later records (from 1967) can be found in FCO 50: Foreign and Commonwealth Office: General and Migration Department.

BRITISH NATIONALITY AND STATUS OF ALIENS ACT, 1914.
CERTIFICATE OF NATURALIZATION

Whereas

Ernst Freud

has applied to one of His Majesty's Principal Secretaries of State for a Certifica
of Naturalization, alleging with respect to   self the particulars set out below
and has satisfied him that the conditions laid down in the above-mentioned Act f
the grant of a Certificate of Naturalization are fulfilled in   case :

And whereas the said   **his**
has also applied for the inclusion in accordance with sub-section (1) of section fiv
of the said Act of the name   of   **Ernst Freud**   child   born before the date of th
Certificate and being   minor **his** and the **ren** Secretary of State is satisfied that t
name   of   child   **ren**, as hereinafter set out, may properly be included :

s Now, therefore, in pursuance of the powers conferred on him by the said Ac
the Secretary of State grants to the said

this Certificate of Naturalization, **Ernst Freud** and declares that upon taking the Oath of Allegianc
within the time and in the manner required by the regulations made in that behalf
shall, subject to the provisions of the said Act, be entitled to all political and oth
rights powers and privileges, and be subject to all obligations duties and liabilities, t
which a natural-born British subject is entitled or subject, and have to all intents an
purposes the status of a natural-born British subject.

And the Secretary of State further declares that this Certificate extends t
the following minor child   of the said
ren
                                        Ernst Freud :-

Stephen Gabriel, born 31st July, 1921.
Lucian Michael, born 8th December, 1922.
Clemens Rafael, born 24th hath subscribed 1924. name this   day o

                                        30th

August, 1939.

                              (Sgd.) A. MAXWELL

HOME OFFICE,
    LONDON.   *Under Secretary of State.*

PARTICULARS RELATING TO APPLICANT.

Becoming British

The concepts of nationality and citizenship, and the laws relating to them, have slowly evolved from the Middle Ages to the present day. Originally the concept of allegiance to a particular feudal lord and to that lord's prince was the reality, rather than the more intangible idea of nationality and the nation-state. The king of England, with possessions in both France and England, had subjects who were French and English. However, as continental possessions in France were lost, a clear distinction developed between subjects and non-subjects: those born outside the king's allegiance were aliens.

Early laws

An Act of Parliament of 1351 confirmed that the king's children born outside the realm beyond the sea were his subjects and could inherit, as also were the children of parents who were in the king's service and allegiance. They could inherit land and property in England. This was confirmed by a further Act in 1368. These Acts did not apply to aliens born outside the king's allegiance and therefore over time the processes of denization and naturalization slowly evolved (see below).

The earliest restrictions on aliens, or 'strangers' as they were then often known, related to foreign merchants and craftsmen. Merchants were often restricted as to when and where and in what commodities they could trade. Stranger craftsmen were also restricted as to where they could work and what goods they could produce. Acts of Parliament in 1523 and 1529 regulated craftsmen and artificers and the 1529 Act required them to swear allegiance when given notice by the masters and wardens of the craft and trade guilds and companies.

Denization

Denization was the process of giving protection and certain rights to aliens and foreign subjects, in return for an allegiance to the Crown and an agreement to obey the laws. Denization did not confer the full rights of a native-born subject, as denizens were still taxed as aliens and were not allowed to inherit freehold property. An Aliens Act of 1540 required all foreigners made denizens by letters patent to obey the laws relating to stranger artificers. Denizens were also allowed to lease dwelling houses and shops. Over time the rights granted became standardized, but until the 17th century they could vary in individual cases with very little distinction between denization and full naturalization, except with regard to public office, the franchise and freehold property rights.

An alien or stranger wishing to become a denizen would first petition the Crown. Unfortunately no such petitions survive before 1800; however, King's Bills authorizing grants to be made survive among the records of the Signet Office from 1585 to 1851. When a King's Bill was submitted to the sovereign for signature, it was accompanied by a summary of its contents, known as a docquet, which was signed by the law officer or clerk of the signet responsible for preparing the Bill. The docquet was entered on the Bill near its lower left-hand corner. The clerks of the signet kept registers of these docquets for the purpose of calculating the fees that were due to them. Short summaries of the docquets are in the Signet Office docquet books and there are indexes by name of applicant. Some earlier and later duplicate docquet books created for the information of the Secretaries of State survive in the State Papers for the period from 1541 to 1761.

Naturalization

Naturalization – the granting of full rights and privileges to a foreign-born alien as though he was a native-born subject – evolved slowly. As early as 1295 the king had granted the rights of a native-born subject to an alien by declaring him to be recognized as an Englishman and requiring all others to do the same. There was no formal process at first: the system developed over time, but by the 17th century full naturalization could only be granted by Act of Parliament. A Bill was introduced into the House of Commons or House of Lords and went through all the stages to become an Act of Parliament. Only the wealthy could afford their own personal legislation. As it was an expensive process, groups of individuals were often naturalized together by one Act. Occasionally legislation allowed whole groups to be naturalized quickly, such as the Act for the Naturalization of Foreign Protestants 1708.

The whole process of naturalization was reformed and the process speeded up by the Naturalization Act 1844, from when applicants could present a memorial to the Home Secretary for a grant of naturalization. Memorial records consist of a petition by the applicant and, in most cases, an affidavit supporting the application. Home Office records may include investigations carried out by local authorities concerning the suitability of the candidate. Before any general naturalization legislation was introduced in 1844, and before the Home Office became actively involved in the granting of naturalizations, there were no general requirements to govern the content of the memorial. Following the 1844 Act, every alien who had the intention of becoming a British citizen was required to present a memorial to the Secretary of State giving age, profession or trade and duration of residence. Following a further Act in 1847, the regulations provided that a declaration should be made and signed by at least four householders, who should state their places of residence, vouch for the respectability and loyalty of the applicant, and verify the several particulars stated in the memorial. The house-holders, known as resident referees, were required to make their declarations before a magistrate. Resident referees were accepted only if they met the following criteria: they were natural-born British subjects; were not the agents or solicitors of the applicant; were able to testify to the facts of residence from personal knowledge; and had known the applicant for at least five years.

The Naturalization Act 1870 required further information, introducing a qualification period for applicants – they should have resided within the United Kingdom for at least five years before submitting an application – in addition to declaring their intention to reside permanently in the country. After 1870, the memorial includes the

Spotlight: Henry James and Raymond Chandler

There are over 2,200 background papers relating to naturalizations of US citizens resident in the UK between 1844 and 1933. Included are several famous cases, such as Henry Solomon Wellcome, founder of the Wellcome Institute; Sir Henry Morton Stanley, who located Livingstone in Africa; Sir Hiram Stevens Maxim, inventor of the Maxim gun; Viscount William Waldorf Astor, MP, owner of the Waldorf Astoria hotel; and Charles Urban, a pioneer of cinematography.

Also included are the files of the literary novelist Henry James and the crime writer Raymond Chandler. Although living in England for many years, James naturalized in 1915, just one year before his death. His papers at the National Archives (HO 144/1429/290366) show that among those he used as a reference supporting his application was the then prime minister, Herbert Henry Asquith. Chandler naturalized earlier, in 1907, though his papers (HO 144/811/136651) show that his naturalization was revoked in 1956 when he chose to become an American citizen again.

name and address of the memorialist, names of any children residing with him or her and the addresses of any residences occupied by them during the preceding five years. From 1880 an additional resident referee was required specifically to verify the dates and addresses and periods of residence required for the five-year qualification period.

After 1873, following communication between the Metropolitan Police Commissioner and the Home Secretary concerning certain Belgians and Germans who had committed offences in their respective countries and who had attempted to apply for naturalization so as to avoid extradition from the United Kingdom, the practice of obtaining a Metropolitan Police report on the respectability of the applicant and the referees was established. Outside London, mayors of municipal authorities and the chairmen of Quarter Sessions were asked to enquire into the respectability of candidates and their referees. The British Nationality and Status of Aliens 1914 Act introduced the requirement for candidates to have an adequate knowledge of English, and memorials after this Act include English proficiency tests.

Discovering the records

Letters of denization
Denizations by letters patent were enrolled on the Patent Rolls now in the National Archives

series C 66. They are indexed in the printed *Calendars of the Patent Rolls* at the National Archives and in large reference libraries. Grants of denization in the Patent Rolls can be found in series C 66 and C 67 until 1844, when responsibility passed to the Home Office (a few later ones appear). To trace an entry for letters patent after 1800 you will need to refer to a series of finding aids to the Patent Rolls and other Chancery Rolls known as Palmer's Indexes, in IND 1/17276–428. These indexes are arranged chronologically and refer to the entries on the Patent Rolls and supplementary Patent Rolls in C 66 and C 67 between 1801 and 1844, when responsibility passed to the Home Office. C 197/29 contains drafts of letters patent of denizations between 1830 and 1873. A few original letters patent of denization are found in C 97, where presumably the patents were not collected by the grantees. With one exception, dated 1830, the original patents in series C 97 all date from the period 1752–92.

Signet Office docquet books recording grants are in the National Archives in series SO 3 for 1585 to 1851. Indexes to the docquet books are in series SO 4 for 1584 to 1851. The Secretaries of State docquets can be found in SP 38, covering 1541 to 1761, with the King's Bills in

SP 39 for 1567 to 1645 and in SO 7 for 1661 to 1851.

No memorial papers survive before 1800. The only records of individual denizations for this period are the letters patent themselves. Between 1801 and 1873 there are three sources of Home Office background papers and memorial papers: HO 1/6–12 for patents issued between 1801 and 1840, HO 44/44–49 for patents issued between 1801 and 1832 (within the HO 44 series list there is a separate index to persons, corporate bodies and places which give folio references within these documents) and HO 45 for letters patent issued between 1841 and 1873. (You simply convert the piece number from the 'OS' – Old Series – number listed in the 'HO number' column.) HO 4 contains original patents of denization, from 1804 to 1843. HO 5 contains out-letters and entry books of the Home Office and the Aliens Office relating to aliens and registers of applications for denization to 1871; out-letters for the period 1871–3 will be found in HO 136.

Acts of Parliament
An Act of Naturalization was obtained by introducing a private Bill into Parliament. Once passed and enacted, it gave the individual or individuals

the same legal standing as a natural-born subject, with full rights of citizenship. The House of Lords Record Office, the Parliamentary Archives at the Palace of Westminster, holds all private Acts of Naturalization. The National Archives has indexes to these private Acts. Abstracts of private Bills of Naturalization are contained in the published House of Lords Journals and House of Commons Journals. Copies of these publications can be seen in the National Archives Library and other major reference libraries. TNA Home Office series HO 1, HO 45 and HO 144 contain some papers and memorials relating to these Bills.

No memorial papers survive before 1800. The only records of individual naturalizations for this period are the individual Acts of Naturalization. There are three sources of memorial papers for this period from 1802 to 1900: HO 1/13–16 for correspondence from 1802 to 1858, HO 45 for correspondence from 1841 to 1878, and HO 144 for correspondence from 1879 to 1900. Note that the years referred to are regnal years counting from the date of the monarch's accession to the throne, e.g. 42 Geo. 3 is 25 October 1801 to 24 October 1802. You can easily convert regnal years to calendar years by consulting C.R. Cheney's *Handbook of Dates*

(Cambridge University Press, 1996) available in the National Archives and in reference libraries and record offices.

The National Archives series KB 24 and E 169/86 include lists of foreign Protestants who, under the Act of 7 Anne, c. 5, in 1708, became naturalized by taking the oaths of allegiance and supremacy in the law courts. These records survive for the period 1708–11. Lists of those taking oaths before the magistrates at Quarter Sessions may survive locally at county record offices in Quarter Session records. From 1740 until 1773, foreign Protestants in the American colonies could also be naturalized by the taking of oaths in court and lists of those naturalized may be found in CO 5 and in the related entry books in CO 324/55–6.

Indexes of denizations and early naturalizations
Indexes to people who successfully secured denization or naturalization during the period up to 1844, published or unpublished, can be found in the National Archives reading rooms located alongside the Home Office series lists, and consist of copies of the following works: W. Page, *Denization and Naturalization of Aliens in England, 1509–1603* (Huguenot Society, vol. VIII, Lymington, 1893); W.A. Shaw, *Letters of Denizen*

*and Acts of Naturalization for Aliens in England,
1603–1800* (Lymington, 1911, Manchester, 1923
and London, 1932, all Huguenot Society); unpublished indexes compiled by clerks in the Home
Office list denizations granted between 1801 and
1873, and Acts of Naturalization from 1801 to
1900.

Naturalization papers and certificates
You can find records relating to naturalization
from the 19th century onwards through Home
Office records held in the National Archives. The
memorials or petitions submitted by individuals
wishing to be naturalized can be found in the
series HO 1/13–176 for the period from 1802 to
1871; HO 45 for the period 1872 to 1878; HO 144
for the period 1879 to 1933; and HO 405 for 1934
to 1948.

You can search the National Archives online
catalogue for background papers to naturalizations from 1844 to 1935 in HO 144, and from
1936 to 1948 in HO 405. The descriptions record
full name, nationality, place of residence and
date of naturalization of applicant. You can also
search the small number of case papers relating
to naturalization by Act of Parliament between
1801 and 1900, and denization by letters patent
from 1801 to 1873.

NATURALIZATIONS AFTER 1922

Memorial papers for naturalizations after 1922 are not available for public inspection. However, don't worry – those for persons naturalized between 1923 and 1948 may be opened under the Freedom of Information Act 2000. Applications are accepted in writing only, but you can submit your request online; having found your reference on the National Archives online catalogue, you can send an email by clicking on the 'Request review' link.

An increasing number of records before 1948 are being opened, but some records will remain closed to maintain confidentiality. Since the basis for closure is usually the personal sensitivity of the information – and this is generally only regarded as sensitive for the lifetime of the individual – researchers who can provide evidence that the individual is dead will be assisting the Home Office considerably in determining whether the file can be opened, although there may, of course, still be continuing sensitivities in regard to other people mentioned in the file.

HO 405 includes those post-1934 applications for naturalization made by people who arrived in the UK before 1948, where the file has survived. This represents an estimated 40 per cent of all such cases so the collection constitutes a very large sample, preserved exceptionally to show the handling of refugees in the period of political turmoil before the Second World War, although there are later files up to 1948.

These records are in the process of transfer to the National Archives in alphabetical order of individual applicant. To date, those for surnames A–N are included on the online catalogue, and it is expected that all the records will be transferred by the end of 2008. Until all the files have been transferred and opened, the Home Office will continue to respond to enquiries from researchers as at present; if files are still with the Home Office, you should address your request to the Departmental Record Officer at the Home Office.

MISSING NAMES

The published indexes and the online catalogue should list all those persons who were successful in securing British nationality from 1509 to 1961, but not all the records to which they refer will have survived. They will only list those who acquired naturalization by Act of Parliament or from 1844 by application to the Secretary of State. They will not include details of women who became British through marriage to a British subject. You should also remember to check variants in spelling or the anglicizing of surnames. If an alien changed their name you will need to check under both the former name and the new name. Until the beginning of 1916 aliens resident in Britain changed their names like British subjects, but from 1916 enemy aliens were then forbidden by Order in Council to change their names. This rule was extended by the Aliens Restriction (Amendment) Act 1919 (as amended by reg. 20 of the Defence (General) Regulations 1939) to all aliens. Exemption was possible only when a new name was assumed by Royal Licence or by special permission of the Home Secretary, or when a woman assumed her husband's surname on marriage. Exemptions in the first two categories were advertised in the *London Gazette*. There are now no restrictions attached to a change of name effected in the United Kingdom by an overseas national. The parts of the Aliens Restriction (Amendment) Act relating to this were repealed by the Statute Law (Repeal) Act 1971. The Defence (General) Regulations had lapsed some years previously.

NATURALIZATION OVERSEAS
Records of individuals who were granted certificates of naturalization by governments of

British possessions overseas can be found in TNA series CO 323, CO 1032 and DO 35 and other relevant CO and DO country correspondence series. Consult A. Thurston, *Sources for Colonial Studies in the Public Record Office* (London: HMSO, 1995) for additional information. Duplicate certificates of naturalization for such cases may be found in Home Office series HO 334 (*see* below). In many cases, duplicate copies of certificates of British nationality granted by colonial governments are housed with British High Commissions. The Foreign and Commonwealth Office website can provide relevant contact details.

Duplicate certificates of naturalization
Copies of the certificates granted to successful applicants after the Naturalization Act 1844 may be found enrolled on the Close Rolls in C 54 for the period from 1844 to 1873, and then duplicate certificates can be found in HO 334 between 1870 and 1987. HO 334 also includes duplicate certificates of declarations of British nationality issued under the British Nationality Act 1948, and these records survive for the period from 1949 to 1987.

Please note that the National Archives does not hold indexes to duplicate certificates after

1980, which are still held by the Home Office Immigration and Nationality Directorate in Liverpool. Permission to see post-1987 certificate records should be sought from the Directorate in Liverpool.

From June 1969 until 1987 the Home Office did not maintain a set of duplicate naturalization certificates (these were the successors to the British Nationality Act certificates). Anyone requiring confirmation of naturalization for this period (often a six-figure reference starting with '0') should write to the Immigration and Nationality Directorate in Liverpool, who will provide a letter of confirmation suitable for legal purposes. This will not, however, add to the information contained in the printed indexes available in the Research Enquiries Room at Kew.

Registration of British citizenship
These documents are generally known as 'R' certificates and refer to registrations of British citizenship declared by a British subject or citizen of the Republic of Ireland or of the Channel Islands, Isle of Man, a colony, a protectorate or a protected state, or a UK Trust Territory.

'R' certificates were issued under the British Nationality Act 1948 and duplicate Home Office copies may be found in the series HO 334. However, the certificates are arranged by certificate number, not by name, and the National Archives does not hold any name indexes to the registration of British citizenship certificates. If you do not have the certificate number, you will need to contact the Home Office Immigration and Nationality Directorate in Liverpool, whose records are arranged alphabetically and give name, date of birth, certificate number and date when the certificate was granted.

The National Archives only holds duplicate registrations of British nationality for those registrations made in the UK and processed by the Home Office, London. Those registered (still prefixed by the various 'R' categories R1–R6) in British possessions and colonies overseas would have been processed by the government of the relevant colony. In such cases, the appropriate British High Commission should be contacted to see if a copy of the registration documentation survives. Contact details of British High Commissioners can be found on the Foreign and Commonwealth Office website.

'R' certificates were issued under the British Nationality Act 1948, and duplicate Home Office copies may be found in the series HO 334. The certificates enabled colonial workers and families to migrate to Britain and settle with ease between 1948 and 1962.

HO 5 includes out-letters of the Aliens Office and the Home Office relating to aliens and registers of applications for naturalization. The series covers the period from 1794 to 1921, although between 1871 and 1873 such out-letters will be found in HO 136. Other out-letters can also be found in HO 43.

Unsuccessful applications

In most cases, files relating to unsuccessful applications for naturalization have not been preserved. Where they survive they can be found, together with departmental papers, in HO 45 between 1844 and 1879 and HO 144 for applications after 1879. There is no complete index to these records and references to any surviving papers may be found in the list relating to the departmental subject heading 'Naturalization' in the main lists for both these series at the National Archives, and not in the separate indexes to naturalizations.

HO 5 series, out-letters and entry books of the Home Office and the Aliens Office relating to aliens, registers of applications for denization and correspondence covering 1794 to 1921,

also includes correspondence relating to unsuccessful applicants. Not all pieces include a
nominal index.

Chapter 4

Refugees in Britain

- Early Protestant refugees
- The Huguenots
- Palatinate refugees
- French émigrés, 1789–1815
- Nineteenth-century refugees
- Belgian refugees, 1914–19
- Jewish refugees from Nazi Germany
- The Czechoslovak Refugee Trust, 1939–75
- Polish resettlement post-Second World War
- Hungarian refugees, 1957
- Discovering the records
  *Huguenots; The French Committee;
  Naturalization of foreign Protestants; Church
  records; Registers of foreign Protestant
  churches; Palatinate refugees; French émigrés
  1789–1815; French Refugee and Relief
  Committee; Polish refugees; Spanish
  refugees; Belgian refugees; Jewish refugees;
  Czechoslovak refugees; Polish resettlement;
  Hungarian refugees*

The Reformation in Europe during the first half of the 16th century saw the first arrival in England of religious, and therefore also inevitably political, refugees. Craftsmen and skilled workmen had usually been made welcome; Henry VIII encouraged certain groups of skilled labourers such as ordnance workers, gunners and armourers from France, Germany and the Low Countries to settle in England, but they were, of course, not leaving their native countries because of religious persecution. This pattern changed over time, however, and more and more of the immigrants were Protestants fleeing Catholic regimes, such as Dutch tapestry-makers, Flemish weavers and glaziers from France and the Low Countries.

Early Protestant refugees

In 1550 Edward VI granted the use of the former Austin Friars Church to the German refugees and other strangers in London. Initially, German, Dutch and French congregations used the church. The congregations were dispersed during the reign of Mary I, but were restored after Elizabeth came to the throne in 1558. The Walloons and French-speaking congregation then obtained the lease of St Anthony's Church in Threadneedle Street, and other communities opened their own churches. One of the earliest nonconformist congregations in England was a foreign community of Walloons who had settled in Southampton, where the authorities had been willing to admit Dutch settlers who had fled from persecution in their own country. Protestants from the Low Countries had petitioned the queen to be allowed to settle in England and carry on their occupations. The harsh rule of Spain in the Netherlands led to an increase in Flemish and Dutch immigration into England, and religious intolerance in France led to the significant arrival of French Protestants, the Huguenots.

The Huguenots

The Huguenots came over in two waves. They fled to England after the massacres on St Bartholomew's Eve in 1572 and continued to do so until the Edict of Nantes in 1598 granted them religious toleration in France. With the revocation of the Edict in 1685, large numbers of Huguenots again fled and settled in England. The main settlements were in London, Norwich, Canterbury, Southampton, Rye, Sandwich, Colchester, Bristol and Plymouth. Their numbers were high and the records of the Privy Council and the Secretaries of State contain many references to them. Such was the public support for them that national collections were made for the refugees in 1681, 1686, 1688 and 1694. Additional money was given by the Crown and later parliamentary grants. The French Committee administered these grants of money for the relief of the refugees.

The number of naturalizations by Act of Parliament increased, and as a result of this Parliament passed a statute in 1708 for the Naturalization of Foreign Protestants (7 Anne c. 5), so that all Protestant refugees who took the oaths of allegiance and supremacy in a court of law, and who could produce a sacrament certificate, were deemed to have been naturalized, without the need for individual Acts of Parliament.

Palatinate refugees

In 1709 large numbers of German refugees from the Rhineland Palatinate and southwestern Germany found a temporary home in London. Most were planning to settle as colonists in North America, but some abandoned this idea and settled in Ireland, in Limerick and Kerry, and were subsidized by the Irish government. Some also settled in the Scilly Isles, and others found employment in the coal mines of the north of England.

French émigrés, 1789–1815

An influx of French refugees between 1789 and 1814, as a result of the French Revolution and the Napoleonic wars, produced much government concern and documentation, resulting in the Aliens Act 1793. The Treasury provided funding for the refugees and aided the Prince de Bouillon as senior naval officer defending the Channel Islands to support the émigrés and gather intelligence on the enemy. The British government also set up a French Refugee and Relief Committee.

Nineteenth-century refugees

In the 19th century, Poles escaping Russian control of their homeland and Spaniards escaping from the Carlist wars in Spain may have seen military service with the British army, and they and their dependants may have become pensioners of the British government. Russian and Polish Jews who fled Tsarist Russia to escape the pogroms settled in the East End of London and other industrial towns. Between 1881 and 1901 some 150,000 immigrants from eastern Europe entered Britain. This influx of poor, often illiterate people resulted in the passing of the Aliens Act of 1905.

Belgian refugees, 1914–19

After the outbreak of the First World War, Britain was called upon to make provision for very large numbers of homeless refugees from Belgium. The War Refugees Committee established a scheme to remove women and children from the theatre of war in Europe and place them under conditions of safe keeping in Britain. The number of refugees from Belgium was over 200,000. A special department was formed at the Local Government Board to deal with all questions relating to war refugees including registration, hospitality, employment, etc. The chief refugee camps were in London at the Alexandra Palace camp, the Earl's Court refugee camp, the Edmonton Refuge and Millfield House. The refugees themselves administered the camps internally. From October 1914 a central register of Belgian refugees was kept. The register recorded a total of roughly 260,000 names. Information about employment and unemployment among the refugees was also obtained, as well as information about Belgians of military age, which was required by the Belgian military authorities. Some

2,500 Local Representative Committees were set up throughout the country and many thousands of refugees were maintained locally. The refugees included a considerable number of Jews, especially from Antwerp, who were cared for by the Jewish Society, later the Jewish War Refugees Committee.

Jewish refugees from Nazi Germany

In the 1930s Jewish refugees began to arrive in the UK from Germany and Austria. Entry was granted predominantly to those refugees who had the prospect of permanent immigration elsewhere. Camps were set up, such as the Kitchener Camp for Poor Persons in Kent, to house Jewish refugees temporarily pending re-emigration to other countries. Over 3,000 Jewish refugees were housed there in 1939. After the *Anschluss* of March 1938, the British government instituted a visa system for German and Austrian refugees in order to stem the possible flow of refugees that might overwhelm voluntary organizations. The British government also began to look for suitable areas of settlement within the Empire. Many of them had been admitted to Palestine, but after 1937 the Peel Commission recommended that no more than 12,000 Jewish

Spotlight: the Freud family

Ernst Freud (1892–1970), son of renowned psycho-analyst Sigmund Freud, and his wife Lucie escaped from Nazi persecution in 1934. Aliens' cards for both of them survive at the National Archives in MEPO 35/29/4 and MEPO 35/29/5 respectively. Ernst and Lucie were both taken off the register on 30 August 1939 when, having resided in the UK for the required minimum period of five years, they successfully became naturalized British subjects. Had they not been classified as such, then, being Austrian, two days later they would have had to sit before an Enemy Aliens Tribunal with the possibility of being interned.

The naturalization certificate in HO 334 (see illustration on p. 42) also includes their children Stephen (the eldest), Lucien (born 1922, the future painter) and Clement (born 1924, the future broadcaster and Liberal MP) as well as Sigmund and Ernst's mother (Martha).

immigrants each year should be admitted for fear of Arab resentment at the arrival of more and more immigrants.

With the outbreak of war in 1939 many Jews, as German nationals, were interned (see also Chapter 6). Tribunals were set up to decide who should be detained and who was to be allowed to remain at liberty. Internment of German and Austrian nationals was dramatically increased from 12 May 1940 onwards. However, this harsh policy was later reversed, and in the period from autumn 1940 to the end of 1942 most internees were released, with many of the remainder who were enemy nationals being repatriated from 1943 onwards.

The Czechoslovak Refugee Trust, 1939–75

The Czechoslovak Refugee Trust was created on 21 July 1939 by deed executed by the Commissioners of HM Treasury, the Home Secretary and three trustees appointed by the Home Secretary. The Trust was wound up in 1975. Its original purpose was the assistance of certain categories of people who sought refuge from Nazi persecution following the ceding to Germany of the Sudetenland under the Munich Agreement of 30 September 1938, and the dismemberment of Czechoslovakia by the Germans in March 1939. These refugees included not only Czechoslovak citizens but also several hundred Germans and Austrians who had fled to Czechoslovakia after escaping Nazi persecution in their own countries between 1933 and 1938.

Before the Trust was created, several appeals had been launched in Britain for subscriptions for the relief of the refugees, among them those by the Lord Mayor of London and the *News Chronicle* and *Manchester Guardian*. Some of this money was set aside for the use in London for the British Committee for Refugees from Czechoslovakia, a voluntary organization set up in October 1938 to provide temporary hospitality in Britain for endangered refugees. British government policy was that the refugees could be accepted in Britain only as transmigrants. Between October 1938 and March 1939 the British Committee brought 3,500 refugees from Czechoslovakia to Britain, and this absorbed all the financial resources of the Committee. In practice the Trust took over where the British Committee left off for lack of funds and when the Czechoslovak government Refugee Department was forced to discontinue operations. The assistance to be afforded to refugees took two forms: emigration to some overseas country of settlement, and maintenance and training in Britain pending re-emigration. In February 1948 a new category of refugees was created following the coup d'état in Czechoslovakia in which a communist regime was established, and the British government enlarged the categories of

Trust beneficiaries to include refugees from that regime.

Polish resettlement post-Second World War

Fighting in North Africa and Europe alongside the British forces were some 160,000 men of the Polish Army. These soldiers were in the main anti-communist, and did not wish to return to a post-war Poland dominated by the Soviet Union. They were brought back to the UK as a serving unit and were re-organized as the Polish Resettlement Corps, which vetted applicants and discharged them from the Polish armed forces. Wives and dependent relatives of these men were then brought to the UK to join them, bringing the total estimated number of cases to over 200,000.

The Polish Resettlement Corps (PRC) was a corps of the British Army, into which Poles were allowed to enlist for the period of their demobilization. The PRC was formed in 1946 and was disbanded after fulfilling its purpose in 1949. The problem of registration, supervision and settlement of the Poles was a huge one, and imposed a great burden of work not only on the Aliens Branch of the Home Office, but also on all police forces throughout the UK. The Polish Resettlement Act 1947 placed upon the Assistance Board the responsibility for meeting the needs, either by cash allowances or maintenance in camps or hostels, of certain classes of Poles and their dependants who had come into the UK since September 1939. Before then, welfare for the Poles had been undertaken by the Polish wartime government in exile until it ceased to function after Great Britain recognized the Polish government in Warsaw at the end of the war. An Interim Treasury Committee for Polish Questions then temporarily administered the welfare for the Poles until the Resettlement Act came into force. The Act enabled the Assistance Board (the National Assistance Board from 1948) to provide accommodation for those whose resettlement was going to take some time to achieve. The Board opened a number of hostels, mainly in the south and southeastern regions of England, providing accommodation for over 16,000 Poles.

The Minister of Education and the Secretary of State for Scotland delegated their powers under Sections 6 and 11 of the Polish Resettlement Act 1947 by setting up, on 1 April 1947, the Committee for the Education of Poles in Great Britain. The Committee, an autonomous body consisting of British and Polish members, had to ensure that the Poles who elected to remain in

Britain would be fitted for resettlement here or in former British territories overseas. This largely involved acquiring an adequate knowledge of English and of the British way of life. Polish institutions maintained by the Committee were eventually dissolved and children and students educated in equivalent British institutions. The Committee was wound up on 30 September 1954. The Minister of Education then appointed an advisory committee to deal with remaining Polish affairs and a Polish section was established in the Ministry. An Education and Library Committee was also set up at the Polish Research Centre to deal with the Polish libraries and adult education in National Assistance Board Hostels. Both these committees were wound up in 1967.

Hungarian refugees, 1957

In October 1956 Soviet forces invaded Hungary following a year that had begun with a gradual controlled de-Stalinization policy, which grew into strong attacks on the communist regime and culminated in mass demonstrations and uprisings among the Hungarian people. The Soviets employed heavy artillery and bombers against the freedom fighters. As the frontier with Austria was, by coincidence, physically open for the first time since 1945 and for a while unguarded, a great flood of refugees poured across it. By the end of 1956 some 153,000 persons had crossed the border, and many thousands, after being given assistance in Austria, found refuge in countries in western Europe and overseas, including Britain.

Discovering the records

Huguenots
The Huguenot Society of London (now the Huguenot Society of Great Britain) has published many records and studies of the Huguenots. The Huguenot Library is a major resource for tracing Huguenot ancestry.

State Papers held in the National Archives should be consulted for material on the Huguenots: in particular, SP 12: State Papers Domestic, Elizabeth I, and later, SP 31: State Papers Domestic, James II and SP 32: State Papers Domestic, William and Mary. These are calendared in the *Calendar of State Papers, Domestic Series*. SP 44 State Papers: Entry Books contains applications for denization, including many for French Protestants. (SP 44/67, in particular, covers the period 1678 to 1688.)

PC 2: Privy Council Registers contains

minutes of proceedings, orders, reports, etc. The volumes are fully indexed and Huguenots should be looked for under French Protestants. From 1670 onwards it is also worth consulting PC 4: Privy Council Minutes and Associated Papers.

The French Committee
The Huguenot Library holds surviving records of this body.

Naturalization of foreign Protestants .
E 169/86 is the oath roll for oaths taken by aliens in the court of the Exchequer from 1709 to 1711. Copies of the sacrament certificates of those naturalized under the statute are in E 196/10. This has been published by the Huguenot Society, vol. xxxv (1932), pp. 11–33.

KB 24/2 contains oaths of allegiance and supremacy taken by persons becoming naturalized under the 1708 Act in the court of King's Bench. These have also been published by the Huguenot Society, vol. xxvii (1923), pp. 72–107, and are described as a naturalization roll (and a duplicate) covering the law terms Easter 1709 to Hilary 1712. Sacrament certificates presented at the court of Chancery may be found in C 224, but there are gaps. Oaths taken locally at Quarter Sessions should be searched for locally among the Quarter Sessions records in county record offices.

Church records
The French Protestant Church of London has its own library and holds its own registers and other records. The London Metropolitan Archives has a collection of Huguenot Society publications (LMA Information Leaflet No. 24) and collections of material on Huguenot businesses and individuals.

Registers of foreign Protestant churches
RG 4: Registers of Births, Marriages and Deaths surrendered to the Non-parochial Registers Commissions of 1837 and 1857, and now held in the National Archives, contains registers of the Walloon and French Protestant churches in England and the French Chapel Royal at St James's Palace (*see* Chapter 12). These records are available on microfilm at the Family Records Centre and at the National Archives, Kew.

Palatinate refugees
Lists of some of these refugees arriving in London can be found in the National Archives in T 1/119, which gives names of individuals and the number of dependants.

French émigrés 1789–1815
The National Archives series T 50: Treasury: Pay Lists and other Documents concerning Refugees contains some material on French ships and expenses of refugees (T 50/57–75).

The Bouillon Papers in HO 69 are a collection of papers and letters to Philippe d'Auvergne, Prince de Bouillon, as 'Administrateur des Secours Accordes aux Emigres'. From 1794 to 1815 he was senior naval officer in Jersey, defending the Channel Islands but also gathering intelligence and supporting French royalist refugees who had fled to Jersey. He was supported by the British government, which provided aid for the refugees. The most relevant papers relating to émigrés are in HO 69/33–8. Other papers of the Prince de Bouillon concerning military matters and the defence of the Channel Islands can be found in HO 69, FO 95 and WO 1. There are also two registers of refugees in Jersey dated 1793 to 1796 (FO 95/602–603). Privy Council records also contain some of his papers (PC 1/115–22, 134–5 and 4490–516). A detailed list of these papers can be found in the non-standard finding aids, which are arranged in series order on the open shelves in the Research Enquiries Room in the National Archives at Kew.

The papers of Charles Alexandre de Calonne, Controller General of France 1783–7, who lived in exile in England from 1787 to 1790 and 1793 to 1802, mainly relate to commercial and political matters and can be found in Foreign Office (FO 95/630–53) and Privy Council records (PC 1/123–33 and 4517). A detailed list can be found with the Bouillon list in the non-standard finding aids.

French Refugee and Relief Committee
The National Archives series T 93: French Refugee and Relief Committee: Records covering the period 1792 to 1823 contains lists of names of those receiving pensions. There are accounts, letter books, memorials and pension lists for the relief of laity and clergy. This series also includes accounts and vouchers for French Protestant refugees from 1813 to 1828.

At the British Library, the Egerton Mss 2728–2832 Account Books relate to this fund for Protestants for the years 1794 to 1836.

Polish refugees in the 19th century
Allowances paid to Polish refugees can be found in the National Archives series PMG 53: Allowances to Polish Refugees and Distressed Spaniards (PMG 53/2–8). The registers are each

indexed and they cover the period 1860 to 1899. The allowances ceased on the death of the last surviving Polish pensioner in 1899. There are also pay lists for the Poles from 1841 to 1856 in series T50/81–97.

Spanish refugees in the 19th century
TNA series PMG 53: Paymaster General's Office: Allowances to Polish Refugees and Distressed Spaniards contains indexed registers of allowances to Spaniards (PMG 53/1–9) from 1855 to 1909. The allowances ceased on the death of the last Spanish pensioner in 1909.

Belgian refugees 1914–19
The National Archives series HO 45 contains some papers under the subject headings, 'Aliens', 'Nationality' and 'War'. HO 45/10738/261921 provides background history of the Home Office's dealings with Belgian refugees. MH 8: War Refugees Committee consists of minutes, history cards, hostel lists, statistics, correspondence and other documents selected from among the records taken over by the Local Government Board from the voluntary committee which administered relief from public funds to Belgian and other refugees. For Belgian refugees 1914–19, there is a considerable amount of

material entered on the history cards. Each card relates to a whole family, unless the refugee was single. The details given are names, ages, relationships, wife's maiden name, allowances and the address for payment. Local Representative Committee records may be found in local record offices.

Jewish refugees from Nazi Germany
The London Metropolitan Archives holds records of the refugees who settled in or around London and were assisted by the Jewish Temporary Shelter. Personal files of approximately 400,000 Jewish refugees are still kept by the Jewish Refugees Committee. Other information on Jewish immigrants is available at the Hartley Library at the University of Southampton, and at the Manchester Local Studies Unit. Access to some records may be restricted.

The National Archives holds records in series HO 396 of the internment tribunals set up from 1939. The records, which date from 1939 to 1947, are in individual binders, usually grouped by nationality, and are in alphabetical order within each binder. The papers may be the original slips, giving personal details on the front and sometimes details of the individual's case on the reverse side (for those interned this information is closed and you would need to request a review of the record). There are also many copy slips within the sets, particularly those listing internees sent out to Canada or Australia. These give name, date of birth, reference and the name of the internee ships with dates of embarkation. Individual internees may have slips in several sets of binders; for example, one person may have been interned in the UK, shipped to Canada or Australia, and finally released from internment and returned to this country, all of which may be detailed in several different pieces. Digital images of all of HO 396/1–106 are available on the Moving Here website. Searches can be made by name of individual alien who was considered for but exempt from internment.

The Moving Here website includes in-depth resources, including exhibitions, galleries and online records both within and outside the National Archives, celebrating Jewish migration to England. The online records include many alien internee tribunal cards for Jewish migrants in series HO 396.

A selection of Home Office files on refugees who did not settle in the UK for the period 1934–48 are in the process of being transferred to the National Archives from the Home Office into series HO 405, and these include records relating to Jewish refugees. Similarly, MEPO 35: Metropolitan Police: Aliens Registration Office: Sample Record Cards includes a heavy concentration of cases around the late 1930s, as Germans and east Europeans fled the Nazis. These cards should be available to download from the National Archives website in 2007.

Czechoslovak refugees 1938–9
Records of the Czechoslovak Refugee Trust are in the National Archives series HO 294. HO 294/1–234 are files relating to policy and administration of the fund. Specimen personal files of refugee families in the various categories are in HO 294/235–486. Case papers of other refugee families, extracted from files that have not been preserved, are in HO 294/487–611: in many instances these provide a detailed case history. A numerical index to cases (HO 294/612–13) is open to readers, but the family files and case papers are not open to public inspection, but a review can be requested.

Related files may be found in FO 371, T 210 (Czechoslovak Financial Claims Office: Files), HO 213 and HO 352/139–40. Also, personal files for some of the staff have been selected for HO 382 (Aliens: Personal Files). These records reveal the political and personal conflicts within the organization and are currently being prepared for transfer. In view of the personal information they contain, it is likely that they will be subject to extended closure periods.

MEPO 35 (Metropolitan Police: Aliens Registration Office: Sample Record Cards) includes a heavy concentration of cases around the late 1930s, which will include Czechs. HO 405 (Naturalization Papers) will include files of those who took out naturalization.

Polish resettlement
The National Archives holds records of the Polish Resettlement Corps (PRC) in WO 315 (Army Records Centre (Polish Section): Polish Records, 1939–50). Note that some of the records are in Polish, although for ease of administration English translations were provided in most cases. The records relate mainly to administrative and policy issues such as organization and disbandment, though WO 315/8 consists of PRC army lists and nominal rolls. WO 315/13–14 are records relating to nursing officers in Polish military hospitals and PRC medical officers, dentists and field ambulance officers.

Assistance Board Records AST 18: Polish Resettlement, Registered Files (PR Series) contains a selection of files dealing with the problems arising out of the Polish Resettlement Act 1947. The records in AST 18 reflect the nature of the administrative work of the board and the camps. Related records can be found in AST 7/939, 953, 1053–4, 1063, 1254, 1255, 1456–9 and 1909.

Education Records ED 128: Committee for the Education of Poles in Great Britain (Gater Committee) and Ministry of Education, Polish Sections of Awards and External Relation Branches: Polish Resettlement Files records the work of the Board and Ministry of Education with regard to Polish resettlement. The series includes awards to successful students with questionnaires and life sketches. Previously closed for 75 years, these records (ED 128/42–75) were opened in 1997 following a re-review. The series includes files relating to Polish institutions in Scotland.

Welfare Records in series LAB 26: Welfare Matters consists of files relating to general welfare matters and includes records relating to housing estates for Polish workers (LAB 26/187–98 and LAB 26/231).

MEPO 35: Metropolitan Police: Aliens Registration Office: Sample Record Cards includes cases around the 1940s, which will include Poles. HO 405: Naturalization Papers will include files of some of those who were naturalized.

Hungarian refugees 1956–7
The National Archives series HO 352: Aliens, General Matters (ALG Symbol Series) Files relates to general establishment matters, policy and casework of the Aliens Department. HO 352/141–9 are files relating to the admission, residence and employment of Hungarian refugees. Over 21,000 refugees entered the UK between 1957 and 1958, though 6,000 went on to Canada and 1,800 chose to return to Hungary. Files concerning the maintenance of Hungarian refugees can be found in AST 7/1621–3. LAB 8/2344 and LAB 8/2371 detail employment arrangements for Hungarian refugees.

Chapter 5

Aliens in wartime

- Internment in the UK during the First World War
- Internment in the UK during the Second World War
- Discovering the records: First World War
  Enemy aliens
  Foreign Office records
  Policy documents
  Individual records
  Record subject areas
  Other sources
- Discovering the records: Second World War
  Home Office personal files
  Applications for naturalization
  Aliens resident in London
  Internees shipped overseas
  Prisoners of war
  Colonial records
  Payment for Far East prisoners of war
  Channel Islands
  Other sources

During both the First and Second World Wars resident enemy aliens were interned by the British authorities, as were British subjects resident in enemy territories.

Internment in the UK during the First World War

Following the outbreak of war against Germany and Austria, the Aliens Registration Act (4 & 5 Geo. V, c. 12) made it mandatory for all aliens over the age of 16 to register with the police. By 9 September 1914, 50,633 Germans and 16,104 Austrians had registered, and those who were considered suspect were interned. By the spring of 1915, following Zeppelin attacks and riots against shops that employed or were managed by Germans, there was a call to intern all enemy aliens between the ages of 17 and 45; this age limit was later raised to 55. By the end of 1915, some 32,274 Germans and Austrians had been interned in camps set up throughout mainland Britain and the Isle of Man. Most were not released until the end of hostilities in 1918.

Internment in the UK during the Second World War

Upon the declaration of war on 3 September 1939, some 70,000 UK resident Germans and

Austrians became classed as enemy aliens. By 28 September, the Aliens Department of the Home Office had set up internment tribunals throughout the country, headed by government officials and local representatives, to examine every UK registered enemy alien over the age of 16. The object was to divide them into three categories: Category A, to be interned; Category B, to be exempt from internment but subject to the restrictions decreed by the Special Order; and Category C, to be exempt from both internment and restrictions. Some 120 tribunals were established, many within London, where large numbers of Germans and Austrians resided. Eleven were in north-west London alone. The police were responsible for providing the details of enemy aliens to the tribunals as they kept registers of aliens, a requirement of the 1914 Aliens Registration Act (4 & 5 Geo. V c. 12).

By February 1940 nearly all the tribunals had completed their work, assessing some 73,000 cases. The vast majority (some 66,000) of enemy aliens were classed as Category C. Most, but by no means all, of the 55,000 Jewish refugees who had come to the UK to escape Nazi persecution in the early and mid-1930s found themselves in this category. Some 6,700 were classified as Category B and 569 as A. Those classified in

Category A were interned in camps across the UK, the largest settlement of which were on the Isle of Man (*see* illustration on p. 90) though others were set up in and around Glasgow, Liverpool, Manchester, Bury, Huyton, Sutton Coldfield, London, Kempton Park, Lingfield, Seaton and Paignton.

However, by May 1940, with the risk of German invasion high, regardless of their category classification a further 8,000 Germans and Austrians resident in the southern strip of England found themselves interned. Following Italy's declaration of war on Britain on 10 June 1940, some 4,000 resident Italians who were known to be members of the Italian Fascist Party, and others aged between 16 and 70 who had lived in the UK for less than 20 years, were ordered to be interned.

The increase in numbers of those interned led to a serious space problem within the UK and, following offers from the Canadian and Australian governments, more than 7,500 internees were shipped overseas on 24 June and 1, 2, 4 and 10 July 1940 on the vessels *Ettrick, Sobieski, Duchess of York, Dunera and Arandora Star*. Tragically, on 2 July 1940 the *Arandora Star* was torpedoed and sunk in the Atlantic en route to Canada. On board were 712 Italians, 438

Spotlight: Lord Weidenfeld and Frank Berni

Several well-known names can be found at the National Archives among records of the Aliens Internment Tribunal card in HO 396, including the publisher Lord Weidenfeld (of Weidenfeld and Nicolson fame). Born Arthur Weidenfeld in Vienna on 13 September 1919, he emigrated to the UK in 1938 and worked for the BBC as a foreign announcer. His internment tribunal card, available on Documents Online, shows that he escaped actual internment because he was a refugee fleeing Nazi persecution and because his profession was likely to help in the war effort.

Not so fortunate was Frank Berni, who in the 1950s was to found, with his brother Aldo, the Berni Inns chain of steakhouses. Born in Bardi, Italy, on 30 October 1903, he emigrated to Wales in the 1920s to join his father's café business, before the family moved to Devon in the 1930s. As an Italian national, Berni was interned in 1940. In addition to his internment tribunal card in HO 396 there are rare surviving transcripts of his internment tribunal among his alien papers in HO 405/2103. This fascinating set of papers also includes detailed reference to his life, from his arrival in the UK to his eventual naturalization in the 1940s.

Germans (including Nazi sympathizers and Jewish refugees) and 374 British seaman and soldiers. Over half lost their lives. It was this event that swayed public sympathy towards the enemy aliens.

The release of 1,687 Category C and B enemy aliens was authorized in August 1940, and by October about 5,000 Germans, Austrians and Italians had been released following the publication of Home Office Under-Secretary Osbert Peake's White Paper *Civilian Internees of Enemy Nationality*, which identified categories of persons who could be eligible for release. By December 8,000 internees had been released, leaving some 19,000 still interned in camps in Britain, Canada and Australia. Of those released, 1,273 were men who applied to join the Pioneer Corps. They would be joined by internees in Canada and Australia, but here the process of release would take longer. By March 1941, 12,500 internees had been released, rising to over 17,500 in August, and by 1942 fewer than 5,000 remained interned, mainly on the Isle of Man.

Unlike for the First World War, the National Archives has a wealth of information relating to internment and internees during the Second World War. These include papers relating to the policy of internment, individual internees and the camps in which they were interned.

Discovering the records: First World War

Unfortunately, very few official records survive relating to internment during the First World War. Some were destroyed during statute in the 1930s; others were destroyed by enemy action during the Second World War.

Enemy aliens
Lists of names of internees were routinely forwarded to the Prisoners of War Information Bureau in London, which in turn informed the International Red Cross Headquarters in Geneva. The lists compiled by the Bureau were largely destroyed by bombing in 1940. However, two specimen lists of German subjects interned as prisoners of war (POWs) in 1915–16 can be found at the National Archives in WO 900/45 and 46. The list is divided into army, naval and civilian prisoners, and gives the regiment, ship or home address of each prisoner.

A classified list of enemy aliens assessed for internment can be found in HO 144/11720/364868. This document is available on the open shelves in the reading rooms in the National

Archives and is arranged by locality of tribunal; unfortunately there is no name index. Nominal rolls of male enemy aliens of the age of 45 and upwards, submitted to the Secretary of State by commandants of internment camps, are included among a census of aliens in the United Kingdom from 1915 to 1924 in HO 45/11522/287235. Lists of alien enemies detained in lunatic asylums within the Metropolitan Police district can be found in this document.

If you're interested more in the policy relating to internees and internment camps, check the Home Office series HO 45 and HO 144. Both series of records are arranged by subject matter and papers relating to internment and internees may be found under the headings 'Aliens', 'Nationality', and 'War'. HO 45/10946/266042 and HO 45/10947/266042 both relate to administration of internee camps on the Isle of Man.

Other material on internees is in correspondence of the Metropolitan Police in MEPO 2. This includes MEPO 2/1633 which consists of the administration of Islington Internment Camp during the First World War.

Foreign Office records

Foreign Office records also provide information about First World War internment. The series of records FO 383 at the National Archives contains records of the Prisoners of War and Aliens Department, and is one of the series of Foreign Office records arising from, and employing, the Foreign Office central registry system for correspondence for the period from 1906. The records in FO 383 relate to the imprisonment or internment of members of the armed forces, civilians and merchant seamen during the First World War, both allied and foreign, and during the period following the Armistice, leading up to the conclusion of the various peace treaties with the enemy countries in 1919.

The correspondence concerns prisoners and internees in all the First World War theatres of war. Apart from relating to the UK, the records are designated according to the countries and territories specified in the FO's correspondence system from 1906 (these are the countries and territories which are stamped on the actual documents and which appear in the first line of the individual catalogue descriptions for each piece). Specifically in FO 383 these countries and territories are as follows: Austria-Hungary, Balkans, Belgium, Egypt, France, Germany, Italy, Netherlands, Russia, Scandinavia, Spain, Switzerland, Turkey, America, and Portugal. There are also references to prisoners and internees in various other countries. These include British dominions and colonies where there were prisoner camps (in particular Australia, Canada, India and South Africa) or internment issues (for example, in Ceylon, New Zealand, Gibraltar, Malta), but also German colonies in Africa and the Pacific, together with other countries in Europe, the Far East, North and South America, Africa and the Middle East.

Several of the prisoner-of-war and internment camps feature prominently in the records, particularly Ruhleben camp near Berlin in Germany. There are papers concerning many other camps and places (including ships) of internment in the UK, such as Donington Hall in Leicestershire, Alexandra Palace in London, Lofthouse Park camp at Wakefield in Yorkshire, the Channel Islands and the Isle of Man (notably Knockaloe camp, and also Douglas), and also overseas, particularly Australia (at Liverpool, NSW), India (at Ahmednagar, near Bombay) and South Africa (at Pietermaritzburg), and others.

Policy documents
At government level, there are high-level policy documents relating to negotiations between the British and German and other foreign governments (through the channel of a neutral foreign

embassy, primarily the USA until they joined the war in 1917) on matters such as the age limits for release or repatriation of prisoners, and reciprocal schemes for the repatriation of sick and injured prisoners. These documents reflect requests to the neutral power to carry out inspections of prisoner camps in both countries, and to ask for investigations into particular cases. These include alleged breaches and violations of the Geneva Convention(s) and the Hague Convention of 1907, and frequent contacts by the Foreign Office with other UK government departments about the advisability of repatriating certain prisoners or the fate of prisoners. There are also papers relating to specific outstanding cases, such as the shooting of the British nurse Edith Cavell.

Individual records
No overall consolidated nominal list of prisoners of war survives, but many FO 383 documents contain lists (of variable size and content) of individuals, including prisoners and civilian internees of both sides. The correspondence in these records originates from a variety of sources. There is a large quantity from the prisoners and internees themselves, as well as from their friends, relatives and other interested parties, such as Members of Parliament and

representatives from neutral consulates who acted as the liaison points between the hostile countries. Requests include those by relatives to send money and food parcels to prisoners; or by firms to send clothing or sports goods ordered by prisoners, or enquiring after the welfare of their interned employees. The mediation of the International Red Cross, the Vatican and foreign royalty is represented, and the work of benevolent institutions and hospital units (often founded and run by society ladies, for example Lady Paget in Serbia), religious groups or trade unions.

Record subject areas
The content of the records is wide-ranging in reflecting many issues relating to imprisonment and internment including:

- enquiries into the welfare or fate of individual prisoners or groups of prisoners, and searches for missing soldiers and individuals in alien countries;
- treatment of prisoners of war; official reports of camp inspections, interviews with escaped or repatriated prisoners, and conditions of prisoners of all nationalities and living conditions in camps (many of which are first-hand accounts by prisoners of their experiences);

- nationality issues, including investigations into proof of nationality of individuals requesting relief and assistance, or from seamen removed from neutral merchant vessels;
- arrangements for the compilation and transfer between governments of lists of prisoners, with many documents containing those lists;
- individual requests for repatriation and financial assistance;
- queries regarding the delivery of letters and parcels;
- censorship of correspondence;
- arrangements for repatriation or transfer of individuals to neutral countries;
- personal papers, including applications for emergency British passports (most of which have photographs of the individuals and details of their family), and some birth, death or marriage certificates;
- investigations into accusations of espionage and contraventions of alien restrictions legislation;
- trade issues, such as trading with the enemy, and firms requesting whether they may supply prisoners of all nationalities with goods;
- communications with missionary societies regarding missionaries in Africa and India;

- property matters, including safety of houses, furniture and personal effects in the belligerent countries, and applications for assistance in recovering luggage and property;
- relief organizations, including activities of the national British Relief Fund and private and charitable schemes;
- Red Cross activities in distributing parcels of food and medical supplies to prisoners, and the transmission of mail between prisoners and their families;
- legal matters, such as transference of powers of attorney, the execution of legal estates following deaths of internees and prisoners, and the disposal of personal effects;
- financial enquiries regarding insurance policies, bank accounts, share dividends, inheritances, pensions, deposits of securities, etc.;
- refugees, including treatment and care of refugees, such as the deportation of Jewish refugees;
- casualties and survivors, including lists and reports from specific campaigns, or from lost ships and submarines;
- visits, including requests by representatives of official and voluntary organizations or other individuals to travel to neutral countries, or foreign subjects to come to the UK;

- consular and diplomatic arrangements;
- minutes and agendas for meetings and conferences of various bodies and inter-departmental committees.

This is not an exhaustive list, and many other associated subjects are to be found amongst the documents. Some documents include reports that are contained in the indexes to the First World War Unregistered Papers in WO 161/101 which do not exist in WO 161/95–100.

Further records relating to PoW camps, administration and policy are found in CO 693, with related registers in CO 754 and CO 755. Records of the Committee on the Treatment by the Enemy of British PoWs (1914–19) are in HO 45/10763/270829 and HO 45/10764/270829, with additional material in WO 162.

Other sources
Other sources survive locally in the localities where internment camps were established. For example, the Manx National Heritage Library holds the island's own records relating to internment on the Isle of Man in both the First and Second World Wars. Other relevant archives can be identified by searching the Access to Archives database.

The Anglo-German Family History Society, a mutual self-help group providing assistance to members in searching for their German ancestors, has done much work in researching records relating to internment and has published useful books on the subject such as *Civilian Internment in Britain during the First World War*.

Discovering the records: Second World War

At the National Archives, the best place for you to start your research is using the series of records HO 396. These consist of index cards for the Internees Tribunals set up in September 1939. The records, which date from 1939 to 1947, are usually grouped by category of aliens exempted from internment or interned, and, for those interned, by nationality. Within categories they are in alphabetical order by surname.

The papers provide personal information on the front such as full name, date and place of birth, nationality, address, occupation, name and address of employer and decision of the tribunal. The reason for the decision of the tribunal for each case is usually noted on the reverse of the card.

The cards have all been microfilmed, and those cases which were deemed as Category B and C and exempt from internment have been made available free as digital images on the Moving Here website. The records can be searched by name, and it is free for you to download images.

The remainder of the series relates to aliens who were at some stage interned and these are available in the Microfilm Reading Room at the National Archives. The reverse of cards for those interned provides information about the time of internment. This information is closed for 85 years, though under the Freedom of Information Act, 2000, it is possible to request a review of the information.

HO 396 also contains information on internees shipped out to Canada or Australia: these give name and date of birth, and the name of the internee ships with dates of embarkation. Individual internees may have cards in several categories; for example, one person may have been interned in the UK, then shipped to Canada or Australia and finally released from internment and returned to this country, all of which may be detailed in several different pieces.

Home Office personal files
You can find further records relating to internees in HO 215. These files deal with individuals interned: chiefly enemy or neutral aliens, but

including a few British subjects detained under Defence Regulation 18B. The papers in this series date from 1940. The Home Office had overall responsibility for the welfare of internees and, from August 1940 onwards, for the internal management and administration of the camps in which they were kept (the War Office retained responsibility for security and the provision of guards). A Home Office personal file would be created whenever the department became involved in the case of a particular internee: when there was correspondence from the camp authorities or from a protecting power, when the internee himself or his relatives wrote to the department or to a Member of Parliament, when an internee was released or died during internment.

The personal case files of internees in the series HO 214 contain a very small sample of the total created, though they do provide you with a picture of how the internees were treated and of the conditions under which they were kept. Most of the files relate to enemy aliens who were interned under the Royal Prerogative; some, however, relate to nationals of friendly countries who were detained under Article Order 1920 (as amended by the Aliens Order 1940) which provided for the detention of any alien considered dangerous or undesirable and who but for the war would have been deported; a few relate to British nationals considered to be of 'hostile origins or association' who were detained under Defence Regulation 18B.

Applicants for naturalization
The series HO 405 relates to individual foreign citizens (mostly European) who arrived in the UK between 1934 and 1948 and who applied for naturalization. All files include application for naturalization with police reports. Some also include initial application for visa or employment permit, change of name or business name and World War II internment papers, as many internees remained in the UK after the war and applied for British nationality in the postwar years. Files were opened when the individual first applied to enter the UK and continue until naturalization or death. All the files in the aliens' personal series were scheduled for destruction, with the exception of a number of illustrative and famous cases which were transferred into HO 382. In 1992 the National Archives learned that not all files opened before 1948 had been destroyed. Those which survived provided suffi- cient additional insight into pre- and postwar European immigration and World War II intern-

ment to justify the preservation of a high proportion. All surviving files which included an application for naturalization have been preserved in this series, regardless of whether the application was approved. It is estimated that some 40 per cent of naturalization applications have survived.

These files are closed for 100 years, though more are becoming open under the Freedom of Information Act, 2000, which allows you to request a review of the information by following instructions on the National Archives' online catalogue. They are currently being transferred according to surname of alien to the National Archives from the Home Office. Those with surnames A–N have been transferred already into HO 405. Those with surnames O–Z are still with the Home Office, and until they are transferred (perhaps by the end of 2008) researchers must contact the Departmental Record Officer at Record Management Services.

Aliens resident in London
Series MEPO 35 contains the surviving aliens' registration cards for the London area. These represent some thousand or so cases out of the tens of thousands of aliens resident in London since 1914. Although the cards represent a small

sample there appears to be a heavy concentration of cases around the late 1930s, as Germans and east Europeans fled the Nazi persecutions. The information provided on the cards includes full name, date of birth, date of arrival into the UK, employment history, address, marital status, details of any children, and date of naturalization, with Home Office reference, if applicable. The cards also include reference to internee tribunals and internment. They usually include at least one photograph and for some cases there are continuation cards. Cards continue until naturalization, repatriation or death.

Internees shipped overseas
Details of internees shipped overseas can be found in BT 27 for outward journeys and BT 26 for return journeys. These are passenger lists of people arriving in and departing from the United Kingdom by sea and were compiled by the Board of Trade's Commercial and Statistical Department. The information given in these lists includes age, occupation, address in the United Kingdom and the date of entering or departing the United Kingdom by sea from or to ports outside Europe and the Mediterranean. The National Archives has received an award from the Heritage Lottery Fund for a project 'Travel to the

UK' to catalogue inward ships' passenger lists in BT 26. The project involves extracting relevant information from the original documents and using the data to improve scope and content in the catalogue related to BT 26, with details of the ship's name, the ship's line, official number, ports of embarkation, and precise date of disembarkation. It is this project that has enabled the recent identification of lists relating to the return of internees from Canada and Australia in 1941. BT 27 will be online by 2008.

There are further papers relating to those interned overseas, including an embarkation list for the *Arandora Star* (HO 215/438), the *Dunera* (HO 215/1), the *Ettrick* (HO 215/267) and the *Sobieski* (HO 215/266).

Prisoners of war
The series HO 215 covers the Home Office and its responsibilities for enemy aliens and (under Defence Regulation 18B) British subjects interned. The series includes reports by the International Red Cross or the protecting power on conditions in British internment camps, and in enemy internment or prisoner-of-war camps. The papers in this series date from 1940 following the institution of mass internment. The Home Office was the Department with overall responsibility

for the welfare of internees and the papers relate to the treatment of internees during their period of internment, the health and educational facilities which they were afforded, their movement within the United Kingdom and abroad, their release and in some cases repatriation, and the conditions in and administration of the camps in which they were kept.

The series contains several examples of reports, by the International Red Cross and by Swiss legations, on the conditions in internment camps in the United Kingdom and the dominions, and also on prisoner-of-war and internment camps in enemy and enemy-occupied countries. The latter were sent to the Foreign Office and forwarded to the Home Office in order that a check could be maintained on the conditions under which British nationals were being held abroad. Camps were often separated into camps for men and camps for women and children.

HO 215 includes nominal rolls of internees in the Hutchinson, Metropole, Mooragh, Onchan and Port Erin camps on the Isle of Man. It also includes lists of repatriation to Germany in 1945.

HO 213 is a broader series, containing policy files relating to the definition of British and foreign nationality; naturalizations; immigration; refugees, internees and prisoners of war; the employment of foreign labour; deportation; the status of citizens of the Irish Republic; and related subjects. There are also papers relating to departmental committees, statistics, conferences, conventions and treaties on these subjects. It contains fascinating files on internment including the document HO 213/1053, which includes photographs of internees and a report of an inspection of camps on the Isle of Man, focusing on women, children and married couples interned there. The camps would set up their own industries (such as glove-making or farm work) and internees were allowed to create their own entertainment. Many of those interned were artistic, including actors, writers, artists and musicians.

Colonial records

Information about enemy aliens and internees in the colonies can be found in CO 968: Defence: Original Correspondence, 1941–1965 and CO 980: Prisoners of War and Civilian Internees Department, 1941–1953.

CO 968 contains records of the Defence Departments, comprising files dealing with all aspects of the defence and security of the colonial empire including matters of policy and internal security. CO 980 contains files of the

Prisoners of War, Civilian Internees and Casualties Department. A large part of this collection of papers concerns civilian internees detained when Singapore and Hong Kong were invaded by Japan. There are also files on the conditions in internee camps. Notable documents within this series include CO 980/119: Lists of civilian internees in camps in the Far East, 1942–1946; CO 980/131: Red Cross lists of British Colonial prisoners of war and civilian internees in Germany and Italy, 1943–1944; CO 980/203: Nominal roll of Colonial merchant seamen interned in Germany and Japan, 1944; CO 980/208: Official Japanese lists of British civilians who died in internment camps in Malaya, 1943–1946; and CO 980/230: Nominal roll of civilian internees released from Stanley camp, Hong Kong, 1945. There is a separate series of registers of correspondence to this series in CO 1012. Some records within CO 980 are closed for 75 years.

Payment for Far East prisoners of war
On 7 November 2000, the government announced a single ex-gratia payment of £10,000 to be paid to the surviving members of the British groups who were held prisoner by the Japanese during the Second World War. The scheme is administered by the War Pensions Agency (WPA);

contact them for information and to request a
claim form. Many of the above series of records
have been requested back by the War Pensions
Agency to enable them to confirm entitlement.

Channel Islands
Records of British personnel interned in the
Channel Islands following the German invasion in
1940 are found in HO 144/22920: Channel Islands:
Evacuation of Channel Islands and German
occupation: lists of people deported to Germany.

Other sources
Local county archives also hold records relating to
internment camps and internees. The Access to
Archives database contains catalogues des-
cribing archives held throughout England and dating from the 900s to the present day. The Manx
National Heritage Library holds the island's own
records relating to internment on the Isle of Man
in both World Wars. Finally, contact the Anglo-
German Family History Society for information on
people from the German-speaking parts of
Europe who have emigrated over the centuries
and settled in the UK and the Anglo-Italian Family
History Society for information about Italian
internees.

References to individual internees and to the

internment camps may be found in the printed indexes of the general correspondence of the Foreign Office, available in the Research Enquiries Room at the National Archives at Kew.

Other Foreign Office records relating to British citizens resident overseas and interned by the enemy forces are in FO 916: Consular (War) Department, later Prisoners of War Department: Registered Files (KW and RD Series), 1939–1948. This series contains registered files of the Consular (War) Department, later the Prisoners of War Department, and comprises reports on prisoner-of-war and internment camps in enemy and enemy-occupied countries and on the treatment of British subjects both military and civilian, and include welfare, exchange, repatriations, escapes and deaths. Various lists of British subjects interned in camps in the Philippines, Hong Kong, Japan, Manchuria, Siam, China and the Dutch East Indies survive within this series.

Later reports are in WO 224: War Office: International Red Cross and Protecting Powers (Geneva): Reports concerning Prisoner of War Camps in Europe and the Far East, 1941–1947. This series consists primarily of a collection of reports dealing with conditions and events in various prisoner-of-war camps in Europe and the Far East.

Beyond the seas

The 19th and early 20th centuries were the great age of passenger travel at sea, and with the development of sea transport came a massive expansion of emigration. The United States was the primary destination, with many seeking to escape war, poverty and religious and political persecution in search of a better life. Canada and Australia also attracted millions. The dream of the emigrant was one of arrival in a country where – so it was said – land was free and fertile, religious and political dissent was tolerated, and class division did not exist.

The growth of sea travel

Shipping companies were initially more interested in transporting mail and merchandise between Europe, America and imperial possessions in India and Africa than in carrying passengers. This was a sideline, and although fares were cheap, conditions were crowded and death from disease was common.

However, it was soon realized that good passenger facilities brought status and increasing custom and large liners were built to transport emigrants, with first-class conditions on the upper decks for the wealthy, and 'steerage', with communal cooking and living arrangements on the lower decks, for the poor. The 1855 Passenger Act also helped to improve conditions, laying down minimum standards for rations, space and sanitation.

Between the 1840s and the 1930s, the fiercely competitive and lucrative transatlantic trade grew rapidly, with the rise of famous shipping lines such as Cunard, the Peninsular & Oriental Steam Navigation Company (P&O), the American White Star Line, the Norddeutscher Lloyd Line and the French Compagnie Général Transatlantique (CGT). Their success rested on a combination of goods and mail transportation, tourism and migration.

In the 1860s steamships started to replace sailing ships, cutting the length of the journey time to North America from over four weeks to about eight days and to Australia from 10–17 weeks to 4–6 weeks.

From the middle of the 17th century, Liverpool was a major port for emigration to North America. Passengers, some of whom were indentured servants, others simply emigrants seeking a better life elsewhere, were attracted to Liverpool from throughout the British Isles (not just the north west of England). Later, in the 19th century, with the attraction of North Sea steamers and railway links across England, Liverpool attracted emigrants from mainland Europe who would travel from the ports of Hamburg or Bremen to Hull and then make their way across to Liverpool by train to board a ship for America. By 1851, Liverpool was the prime migrant port of Europe, sending approximately 160,000 passengers to America in that year alone; during the period 1830 to 1930 over 9 million emigrants left Liverpool in search of a new life. By the 1860s, Liverpool had begun regular voyages to Australia and New Zealand, though these destinations proved popular from other UK ports, particularly London and Southampton and, to a lesser extent, Bristol.

Cunard, White Star, Allan, Inmar, Guion and National Lines all sailed from Liverpool, though many refused to carry passengers until the 1860s.

By the late 19th century, Liverpool's dominant role was being challenged – particularly by German ports, such as Bremen and Hamburg, but also by Southampton. The position of Liverpool was further weakened in 1926 when restrictions on immigration were imposed by the USA. Following this, other destinations such as Canada and Australia became increasingly popular, encouraged by governments both in the UK and in the Dominions and the Commonwealth.

Spotlight: Bob Hope and Cary Grant

At the National Archives, the Board of Trade Passenger Lists: Outwards (BT 27), 1890–1960, contain the names of some 30 million people leaving the United Kingdom from ports within England, Wales, Scotland and Ireland for final destinations outside of Europe and the Mediterranean. The series is undergoing digitization as part of an initiative to place it online and make it fully searchable by passenger name, ship name, port and date (completion due in 2008.)

Among these millions are many who made their fame and fortune in America. One such was the five-year-old, London-born Leslie Hope (1903–2003), who arrived in New York travelling from Southampton on the SS *Philadelphia* in March 1908 with his mother and five brothers (BT 27/594). In later life he would achieve iconic status as the actor and entertainer Bob Hope.

Similarly, 16-year-old Archibald Leach (1904–86) emigrated from Southampton to New York in July 1920, on the SS *Olympia* (BT 27/931). Donning the stage name Cary Grant he would become a Hollywood legend, acting in films by Alfred Hitchcock (another expat) and others.

Discovering the records

Surviving documents (published and unpublished) used to record the departure of emigrants are listed below. British outgoing passenger lists are usually less fruitful in terms of family history information than those 'incoming' lists kept overseas. Also, unlike some overseas archives, there are no outgoing passenger lists in the National Archives for civilian aircraft.

Many outwards passenger lists to America, Australasia and South Africa have been published, particularly those that date before 1800. Some publications have been compiled from primary sources within the National Archives but most have been published using sources recording the arrival of emigrants in the destination countries. A number of known publications are listed at the end of the book; many of these are available in the Research Enquiries Room or Library and Resource Centre at Kew. Many are particularly rich in source material. For example, Filby and Meyer (eds), *Passenger and Immigration Lists Index* is effectively a guide to published records of more than 3,340,000 immigrants who travelled to the New World between the 16th and mid-20th centuries. Entries within these volumes have been derived from a broad collection of more than 1,080 published passenger lists, naturalization records, church records and local histories, together with electoral lists and land registration records.

Most of the records of passengers leaving the UK are scattered among a variety of archives or have simply not survived. However, much material can be found at the destinations where the passengers became new citizens.

Generally speaking, emigration passenger lists between 1776 and 1889 have not survived. For the period before 1820, the Genealogical Society of Baltimore, USA, has reprinted all the surviving lists for vessels bound for North America and these include those for 1773–6 in T 47, as well as much of the material found at the destination ports in America. The National Archives holds most of these listings.

Passports and licences to pass beyond the seas, 1573–1948
You'll find that information held in the National Archives on individual passport-holders is scanty; the National Archives does not hold completed application forms, except for a small sample illustrating the treatment accorded to applications of various types, and there is very little genealogical information in the bulk of these records.

Passports were not compulsory for travel overseas until 1915, and before this time it was rare for someone travelling abroad to apply for a passport.

LICENCES TO PASS BEYOND THE SEAS

Until the 17th century, the monarch had the prerogative right to control the movement of his subjects overseas, and records of applications for and grants of permission to leave the kingdom are to be found in the series of records E 157: Licences To Pass Beyond The Seas. The records in this series consist of two main types: first, registers of people taking oaths of allegiance before leaving the realm, and second, registers of licences to pass beyond the seas. The earliest records in this class date from 1573, although regulation of travel existed before this time. The bulk of the registers come from 1613–35, with an odd one from 1677. From 1610, all people over the age of 18 travelling abroad were required to take an oath of allegiance, according to the statute 7 James I, c. 6. From 1637 no passengers could go to the American colonies without a licence from the Commissioners for Plantations.

Most entries concern details of soldiers taking the oath of allegiance before going to serve in the Low Countries between 1613 and 1633, though some include other people going to continental Europe, chiefly to Holland, between 1573 and 1677. There are also a few, rather unexpected, registers of people travelling to Ireland and Scotland (E 157/17, 24 and 31). The entries generally include date, name and destination, and sometimes age and place of residence.

Similarly, the series SP 25: State Papers: Books and Accounts, includes passes and warrants to go abroad; SP 25/111–116 in particular consist of passes, mainly for Europe for 1650–60. Entry books of passes issued by the Secretaries of State between 1674 and 1784 are in the State Papers, SP 44/334–413. A further entry book of passes, some signed by the king, between 1748 and 1794 is FO 366/544. Earlier entries usually give an abstract or copy of the pass, but from January 1793 there is merely a name and a date and there is no nominal index. SP 44: State Papers: Entry Books: Warrants and Passes, 1661–1828, includes, in SP 44/386–413, passes for aliens going abroad and for merchants to trade overseas giving details such as name of ship, burden, master, cargo, ports of departure and destination, and period of validity, 1697–1784. The records are indexed to 1722 and described in *Calendar of Home Office Papers in the Reign of George III, 1760–75*, available in the Map and

Large Document Room at Kew. These passes were issued to prevent the return from the Continent of persons under attainder for the plot against William III in 1696.

PASSPORTS

The main series of passport registers from 1795 to 1948 are in FO 610 but you may be disappointed with the information – they show merely the date, the number of the passport issued and the name of the applicant. Early registers also show where the applicant was going and by whom he was recommended. Separate registers of passports to Peking, China, 1874–1926, can be found in FO 563 and FO 564; to Germany, 1850–81 in FO 155; to Hanover, 1857–66, in FO 159/28 and 56; to Saxony, 1819–75, in FO 218; to Sicily and Naples, Italy, 1811–60, in FO 166; to Mexico, 1816–1927, in FO 207; to Warsaw, Poland, 1830–1914, in FO 394, and to Barcelona, Spain, 1775–1922, in FO 639.

You can view indexes of names of passport applicants in FO 611. These are on microfilm at the National Archives and cover the years 1851–62 and 1874–1916. For the latter period the index is not strictly alphabetical. There is a section of index, called a cut, for each letter of the alphabet. Within it the names are listed chronologically.

Again, you may be disappointed with the scant information recorded: solely the name, the number of the passport and the date of issue.

The richest records are the small selection of passport representation case papers in FO 737. These illustrate the treatment accorded to applications for various types of passports, visas and certificates, and date from 1920 to the 1970s. You can find colonial applications for passports, 1796–1818, in CO 323/97–116, and thereafter among the Original Correspondence of the colony of issue. A highly miscellaneous sample of passports is kept in FO 655. It includes some passports issued in the late 18th and early 19th centuries by foreign missions in Great Britain to British subjects wishing to travel abroad. This practice ceased in 1858.

Port Books, 1565–1798

Early emigrants are listed among E 190: Exchequer: King's Remembrancer: Port Books, 1565–1798. These were compiled as a result of an Exchequer Order of November 1564 requiring all customs officials in the various ports of England and Wales to make their entries in blank books issued by the Exchequer. The books are of three kinds: entry books of the collectors and other officials, recording the details of cockets issued as receipts for the payment of the various duties on imports and exports; entry books of searchers, waiters and other officials who were concerned with shipping movements and the inspection of cargoes, not with the collection of duties; and coasting books, which record the issue and return of certificates for the transit of goods by coast from one English port to another. The certificates stated that the shippers had entered into bonds to unload only at another port within the realm.

Each entry in a Port Book generally contains the name of the ship and its master, the names of the merchants, a description of their goods, and, in the entry books of the collectors, the amount of duties paid. After 1600 most books contain details of the places to and from which shipments were made. Undoubtedly some of the exporters were also themselves emigrants, but there is no way of distinguishing between the two from the records. The records are not indexed by name though they have been used to compile many of the sources indicated in the bibliography. The records are arranged by port and then by date. The ports named are those that were prosperous and prominent in early modern England and each 'headport', such as Chester, also subsumes a number of other ports, such as Liverpool and Lancaster.

Registers of passengers, 1634–77
You can find several registers of passengers travelling from a number of UK ports to New England, Barbados and other colonies for 1634–9, with one of 1677, in E 157: Exchequer: King's Remembrancer: Registers of Licences to Pass Beyond the Seas. The registers have been printed in J.C. Hotten, *Original Lists of Persons Emigrating to America, 1600–1700*.

Similarly, you can also find lists of passengers, with names and ages, on board vessels bound for America in the 1630s in CO 1: Privy Council and Related Bodies: America and West Indies, Colonial Papers (General Series). These include CO 1/8, folios 100–2 displaying names of passengers bound for New England on board the *Francis of Ipswich* in 1634 and CO 1/9 folios 246–7, which includes names of passengers intended for New England on the *Confidence* in 1636–8.

Treasury registers of passengers, 1773–6
A useful Treasury register (T 47/9–12) was kept by port customs officials of emigrants going from England, Wales and Scotland to the New World between 1773 and 1776. The information for England and Wales has been summarized in a card index, available in the Research Enquiries Room at the National Archives, which gives

name, age, occupation, reason for leaving the country, last place of residence, date of departure, and destination. This series also includes names of passengers to Europe.

Shipping line emigration lists, 1840–1909
The University of Liverpool has in its archives a small selection of outward passenger lists from the Cunard and White Star shipping lines. Very few passenger lists are included in their archive, but those which are cover the period 1840 to 1909 for voyages to Canada and the USA. For example, the university has three microfilms of passenger lists of the Cunard Line for the period 1840–53.

The Merseyside Maritime Museum Library and Archives holds diaries and letters of emigrants, family history notes and other official documents and correspondence, including selected passenger lists and surgeons' reports.

No records of 'exit passes' of passengers or passenger application forms are known to survive in any UK archive.

No shipping line passenger lists appear to survive for the port of London for the period before 1890, although P&O (the Peninsula & Oriental Shipping Line) has lodged its archives with the National Maritime Museum in London.

Hamburg passenger lists, 1850–1934
Your ancestor may have emigrated from mainland Europe via the UK. In such cases, you may need to access lists of passengers on vessels sailing from Hamburg between 1850 and 1934 which survive in the Hamburg State Archive, with microfilm copies available through Latter-day Saints family history centres. There are two types of lists, direct and indirect manifests, the latter of which contain the names of those passengers who proceeded from Hamburg to an intermediate British or other European port, where they boarded other vessels for their ultimate destination, likely to be in North America. The lists extend from 1854 to 1910; the names of such passengers for 1850–4 and from 1911 onwards are included in the direct lists. The information on the manifests includes surname, forename(s), age, gender, previous residence, occupation and destination. A database of names provided by the Hamburg State Archives is now available on the Link to Your Roots website.

Passenger lists to New Zealand, 1839–50
If your ancestors migrated to New Zealand you may wish to consult the series CO 208: New Zealand Company Original Correspondence, 1839–1858. The New Zealand Company was

formed in 1839 and incorporated in 1841 with power to buy, sell, settle and cultivate land in New Zealand. It surrendered its charter in 1850 and was dissolved in 1858. This series of records contains registers of cabin passengers emigrating, 1839–50, in CO 208/269–72; applications for free passage, 1839–50, in CO 208/273–4 (indexed in CO 208/275); applications for land, lists of landowners, in CO 208/254–5; lists of agents and surveyors, lists of German emigrants, and lists of maintained emigrants, in CO 208/ 278–81.

Birth, marriages and deaths of passengers at sea, 1854–1972

Your ancestor may have been born, married or died on board emigrating vessels. There was no legal requirement to list passengers on board British vessels prior to the Merchant Shipping Act 1894, though following the Merchant Shipping Act 1854 registers were compiled, from ships' official logs, of births, deaths and marriages of passengers at sea. (*See also* Chapter 12.)

Most emigrants travelled in the cheapest class of accommodation, known as steerage. It was frequently overcrowded and ventilation was poor; diseases such as cholera and typhus reached epidemic proportions and many emigrants died as a result, particularly prior to the

1870s (by which time virtually all emigrants to North America and most to Australia travelled by steamship, which cut journey times considerably). From about 1900, third-class cabins replaced steerage accommodation, and although they were spartan this was a considerable improvement.

Births, marriages and deaths are all recorded in the National Archives from 1854 to 1883, births and deaths only from 1883 to 1887 and deaths only from 1888 to 1890. You can find these records in the series BT 158: Registers of Births, Deaths and Marriages of Passengers at Sea. Masters were further required by the Registration of Births and Deaths Act 1874 to report births and deaths of both United Kingdom subjects and aliens to the Registrar General of Shipping; the information about United Kingdom subjects is in the series BT 160: Registers of Births of British Nationals at Sea and BT 159: Registers of Deaths of British Nationals at Sea. Records of births and deaths at sea, 1891–1964, are held in BT 334 with a marriage register for 1854–1972.

At the Family Records Centre (FRC) you can search births and deaths at sea (marine) of British people, registered from July 1837 to 1965. Civil aviation births and deaths and missing (presumed dead) from 1947 to 1965 are also available at the FRC. From 1966, all births, marriages and deaths at sea and registered by the UK High Commissions and consuls abroad are indexed in union volumes for each type of event.

Outward Board of Trade passenger lists, 1890–1960

The Merchant Shipping Act, 1894 (57 & 58 Victoria, c. 60) required the listing of passengers on board British merchant vessels. Ships' passenger lists at the Board of Trade relate mainly to arrivals in and departures from UK seaports, including Ireland before 1924. The lists were deposited with the Board of Trade by the various passenger shipping lines. The series BT 27 contains Passenger Lists: Outwards.

FINDING YOUR DOCUMENT

To find your document you should know the first port of departure from the UK and the date of departure. Some ports are not named separately, but included with other ports nearby. Other ports are also known by different names, e.g. Queenstown was also listed as Cork. If you do not know the port of departure but do know the name of the ship, you could use the Registers of Passenger Lists, 1906–51, in BT 32, available on the open shelves in the Research Enquiries Room at Kew. These registers contain names of ships for which passenger lists exist in BT 27, but beware – they are not complete. The earliest years have entries for a few ports only and there are omissions for later ones.

Available at the Research Enquiries Room desk, *The Morton Allan Directory of European Passenger Steamship Arrivals* (Genealogical Publishing, 1993) contains listings of the arrivals of passenger steamships at New York for 1890–1930 and Philadelphia, Boston and Baltimore for 1904–30. The directory is arranged by year and alphabetically indexed by steamship line. The port of arrival and port of departure are shown at the top of each entry. As with BT 32, the *Directory* does not contain the names of passengers but provides clues as to where passengers may have sailed from in a particular year, and is of help if the name of the vessel is already known but the port of departure is not.

The outward lists in BT 27 provide details of all passengers leaving UK ports, where the ship's eventual destination was a port outside Europe and the Mediterranean Sea. However, names of transmigrants and passengers who disembarked at European ports will be included in these lists. Passenger lists for ships whose voyages both began and ended within Europe (including the UK and the Mediterranean) are not included. The information available from these lists varies, but can include age, address in UK (from 1922) and occupation. Lists after the 1930s indicate whether or not passengers were travelling for tourist/leisure reasons using the abbreviation 'T'. There are also separate lists for British and alien passengers.

ONLINE RECORDS
If you do not know the port of departure or the name of the ship, it will be very difficult and time-consuming to find any record in BT 27. Having said this, these records, containing details of over 30 million passengers, will gradually be made available online by the National Archives in partnership with 1837online.com, a project which will run from the end of 2006 until the beginning of 2008. For a fee, the original manifests can be downloaded and will be searchable by name of passenger, name of ship, port or date of departure, and destination. It will be free to download images if you visit the National Archives or the Family Records Centre. Many of the original passenger lists are in a fragile condition, so will not be produced to readers once available online. Also, until they are available online, the originals are being scanned and transcribed, so if you intend to come to the National Archives to view an original passenger list before the project is

completed, it's a good idea to check the availability of the original before you travel. In the meantime and until the online project has been completed, there are further online clues available to help track down passenger lists in BT 27.

The first set of passenger records to be provided on the Origins Network website are abstracts of BT 27 passenger lists from British and Irish ports with US and Canadian destinations. The names of over 100,000 passengers are included, using some of the early lists from the 1890s. These records are currently exclusive to the Origins Network and include date of sailing, ship's name, departure port and destination port. For each passenger, the full name is given, with occupation, nationality, age and marital status.

If your ancestor migrated to Canada between 1925 and 1935, check the Canadian Archives online database. Until BT 27 is available online, this is an extremely valuable resource in helping you identify the outgoing passenger list in BT 27, in conjunction with using registers in BT 32.

If your ancestor migrated to the USA via Ellis Island between 1892 and 1924, check the online USA immigration lists. Again, this can allow you to identify corresponding UK outward passenger lists in BT 27.

Although there are no indexes of names and

most lists are not alphabetical, DataMarine has extracted almost 50,000 names and details from some Board of Trade passenger lists for Australia-bound vessels for the years 1909–14.

Passenger lists held in overseas archives
Seventeen million people have emigrated from the UK and Ireland since the 17th century and some of the richest records relating to their departure are available in the archives of the country of destination. We will discuss this more in Chapters 8, 9 and 10, but here is a summary:

• Australia: you can search inwards passenger lists for all ports in Australia from 1924, with some gaps. Earlier inwards passenger lists survive for the ports of Newcastle (for 1865–84), Darwin (1898–1934), Bowen (1897–1962), Brisbane (1852–1964), Cairns (from 1897), Hobart (from 1903), Rockhampton (from 1898) Townsville (from 1895), Fremantle/Perth (from 1898). Further information is available at the National Archives of Australia website. Inward air passenger lists generally survive from 1934 and, as with the ships' passenger lists, these records tend to be held at the state archives.

• New Zealand: through the Archives New Zealand website you can search passenger lists for ports in New Zealand from 1883 onwards. These lists were compiled by shipping companies and handed to a customs officer when the ship arrived in New Zealand. The amount of information they contain varies, though most lists include the person's surname and initial, age, occupation and nationality.

- Canada: most passenger lists survive for the period 1865 to 1935 and they contain information such as name, age, country of origin, occupation and intended destination of passengers. From 1925 the lists also contain the immigrant's place of birth, the name and address of the relative, friend or employer to whom they were destined, and the name and address of the nearest relative in their departure country. Also the Library and Archives Canada website.

- USA: most passenger lists survive from 1820. Records usually include name of passenger, country or town of origin, date of arrival, destination in the USA, occupation, age and gender. Many of the passenger lists have been indexed though there are important periods where no indexes exist, such as for New York from 1847 to 1897, and for Boston for 1820 to 1847 and again from 1892 to 1901. For such instances, the records are arranged chronologically and by port of arrival. Also check the US National Archives website.

A NOTE OF THE SHIP-
PING, MEN, AND PROVISIONS, SENT
to VIRGINIA, by the Treasurer and
Company, in the yeere 1619.

THe *Bona Noua*, of 200. Tun, sent in August 1619. with ⎬120. persons.

The *Duty*, of 70. Tun, sent in Ianuarie 1619. with ⎬51. persons.

The *Ionathan*, of 350. Tun, sent in Februarie, 1619. with ⎬200. persons.

The *Triall*, of 200. Tun, sent in February, 1619. with ⎬40. persons, and 60. Kine.

The *Faulcon*, of 150. Tun, sent in February, 1619. with ⎬36. persons, & 52. Kine. and 4. Mares.

The *Marchant of London*, of 300. Tun, in March, 1619. with ——200 persons.

The *Swan of Barnstable*, of 100. Tun, in March, 1619. with ——71. persons.

The *Bonauenture*, of 240. Tun, sent in April, 1620. with ——153. persons.

Ships.

Besides these, set out by the *Tresurer* and Company, there haue been set out by particular Aduenturers for priuate *Plantations*.

The *Garland*, of 250. Tun, sent in August, 1619. with ——45. persons. who are yet detained in the *Summer Ilands*.

A Ship of *Bristoll*, of 80. Tun, sent in September, 1619. with ——45. persons.

There are also two Ships in prouiding to be shortly gone, for about 300. persons more, to be sent by priuate Aduenturers, to *Virginia*. ⎬300. persons.

Summe of the persons. ——————1261.

Whereof in the eight Ships set out by the *Treasurer* and Company. ⎬871.

Of these persons there are sent for publicke and other pious vses, these ensuing:

People.

Tenants for the Gouernours Land, (besides fiftie sent the former spring.)–80

Tenants for the Companies Land. ——————130.

Tenants for the Colledges Land. ——————100.

Tenants for the Ministers glebe Lands. ——————50.

Young maids to make wiues for so many of the former Tenants. ——90.

Boyes to make Apprentices for those Tenants. ——100

Seruants for the publicke. ——————50.

Men sent by their labours to beare vp the charge of bringing vp ——50.

Thirty of the *Infidels* children in true Religion and ciuility. ⎬50.

Summe of Persons for publicke vse, &c. ——650.

The 611 remaining, are sent for priuate *Plantations*.

A

The

Chapter 7

Crossing the Pond

- Voluntary and involuntary departures
- Discovering the records: transportation
  Trial records
  Pardons, appeals and petitions
  Transportation lists
- Discovering the records: free emigration
  Colonization of North America
  Land grants
  Hudson Bay Company records
  American Loyalist claims
  Poor Law records
  Missionary records
  Passenger lists

The end of the 16th century saw the beginnings of what, in the next 500 years, would become the biggest migratory trend from Europe: emigration to North America. In 1585 Sir Walter Raleigh established the toehold at Roanoke Island, off present-day North Carolina, but it failed within a few years. In 1607, though, colonists landed to found Jamestown (Virginia) and they survived to begin English settlement of the continent proper. In 1620, alienation from (as they saw it) a repressive Anglican Church and a tainted social world motivated a new kind of emigrant to up sticks and leave in the *Mayflower*. Thus, the Pilgrim Fathers began that association of America with the religious idea of a 'promised land' and a refuge from persecution.

Voluntary and involuntary departures

For the majority who left Britain and Ireland to cross the Atlantic, two other factors would prove decisive: crime and economic well-being.

Beginning in the 17th century and for 150 years afterwards, thousands were sent to the American colonies forcibly, as punishment for their lawbreaking. It is estimated that some 50,000 men, women and children were transported to America and the West Indies between

1614 and 1775. Most were from the poorest class and nearly half were sentenced from courts in or around London. Transportation to the West Indies was generally for no more than 10 years, as most of the islands forbade longer sentences. (Although most transportation to the West Indies took place in 1615–60, between 1824 and 1853 some 9,000 convicts were also sent from Britain to help build the naval and military station at Ireland Island, Bermuda.)

The bulk of migration across the Atlantic, however, related to free emigrants. People rapidly emigrated and populated the New World because of the new sources of revenue it represented, and because of the chance to expand boundaries. And once there, the colonial population was not static. For example, after the American War of Independence, Loyalists left for Canada, Nova Scotia, the Bahamas and England. Also, after the abolition of slavery, emigrants from the Indian sub-continent were encouraged to emigrate to the West Indies to help with local labour problems, as indentured/bonded labour.

It is estimated that since 1607 over 10 million emigrants have left Great Britain and Ireland for the USA, with 4 million to Canada. Between 1845 and 1851 over 1.25 million Irish emigrated to the USA as a result of the Potato Famine.

Spotlight: Charlie Chaplin and Stan Laurel

The British-born actors and directors Charlie Chaplin (1889–1977) and Stan Laurel (1890–1965) emigrated to the United States together, via Canada, on the SS *Cairnrona* in September 1910. Both were then part of Fred Karno's prestigious comedy troupe, and their names are listed in the National Archives on a page with a further 15 actors and actresses (BT 27/688). They had been sent to the United States to perform *Mumming Birds*, a self-reflexive parody of British variety entertainments and the music-hall experience. Laurel is listed under his real name, Stanley Jefferson.

Both, of course, would go on to settle in America and become hugely popular globally, Chaplin as king of silent comedy and co-founder of United Artists, and Laurel as the inimitable comic partner of Oliver Hardy.

Discovering the records: transportation

Trial records

Convicts transported between 1615 and 1718, or transported for 14 years after 1718, would have been convicted in a court of assizes or one with equivalent legal power.

You can consult surviving assize court records at the National Archives. There are various series of records to consult, including indictments and depositions. The records are arranged by assize circuit and chronologically. You may find that some convicts have been tried at the Quarter Sessions. These records are held in local record offices.

Trial records do not usually contain useful genealogical information, nor do they contain transcripts of evidence. They may contain copies of pre-trial witness statements. The indictments were written in Latin, and in a distinctive legal handwriting, until 1733. Pre-trial witness statements are in the ordinary hand of the day, but if you are not familiar with 17th-century handwriting you may find it difficult to read. Sometimes reports of trials were published; the Old Bailey Proceedings, for example, were published from the 1670s onwards, and are available online. This site now contains 101,102 trials, from April 1674 to October 1834. Transcripts and pamphlets about trials in other parts of England and Wales can be traced using the *Eighteenth Century Short Title Catalogue*, compiled by the British Library. This should be available to you at a large local reference library A copy is available in the National Archives Library.

Pardons, appeals and petitions
You should note that not all those who were sentenced to transportation actually went. Some convicts were successful in an application for mercy. Before 1784 reference to such applications may be found among State Papers (SP) Domestic records. *Calendars of Home Office Papers, George III, 1760–1775*, in the Map and Large Document Room at the National Archives, includes lists of criminals with information relating to the crime committed, sentence passed, and the date and location of criminal trial. Original records to which the calendars refer are in SP 44: State Papers: Entry Books, 1661–1828. Earlier records can be found in SP 35: Secretaries of State: State Papers Domestic, George I and SP 36: Secretaries of State: State Papers Domestic, George II. Both series of records contain a large and miscellaneous collection of papers concerning transportation to America. Included here are letters of appeal from convicted prisoners, their friends and families, lists of reprieved felons, and opinions of judges.

You may wish to consult C 66: Chancery and Supreme Court of Judicature; written in Latin, these parchment rolls contain a complete series of pardons from the death penalty on condition of transportation from 1654 to 1717.

Transportation lists
You can find transportation lists from 1747 to 1772 at the National Archives. *Calendars of Treasury Papers, 1557–1728, Treasury Books, 1600–1718* and *Treasury Books and Papers, 1729–1745* are available in the Research Enquiries Room to help identify references in the series T 1.

Similarly, lists can be found in T 53: Treasury: Entry Books of Warrants relating to the Payment of Money. These include records of payment made by the Treasury to contractors engaged in the transportation of felons between 1718 and 1752. Until 1744 the names of all those to be transported from London and the Home Counties, together with the names of the ships in which they were to be transported and the destination American colony, are included in the Money Books. Thereafter, only statistics concerning transported felons are entered, with the names of the transporting ships and their masters.

CO 5: Board of Trade and Secretaries of State: America and West Indies, Original Correspondence, 1606–1822, includes material on all aspects relating to transportation to America and the West Indies. A key finding aid to this series is *Calendars of State Papers, Colonial, America and West Indies, 1574–1738*, available on CD-ROM at the National Archives.

Discovering the records: free emigration

Colonization of North America

The National Archives holds a great deal of material concerning emigrants to all colonies. CO 384: Emigration Original Correspondence, 1817–96, contains many letters from settlers or people intending to settle in British North America, Australia, the West Indies and other places; there are separate registers for British North America. Details of land grants and applications may be found in CO 323: Colonies, General: Original Correspondence, 1689–1952; CO 324: Colonies, General: Entry Books Series I, 1662–1872; and CO 381: Colonies, General: Entry Books Series II, 1835–1872.

The major early collection of papers relating to the West Indies and the American colonies (CO 1) has been described and indexed in the *Calendar of State Papers, Colonial, America and West Indies* (now available on CD-ROM), which includes references to the many other succeeding classes as well. It is also worth searching the following series of original correspondence for North America, together with its related registers in the following series: CO 5: America and West Indies, Original Correspondence, 1606–1822; CO 6: British North America Original Correspondence, 1816–1868; CO 42: Canada, formerly British North America, Original Correspondence, 1700–1922; CO 60: British Columbia, Original Correspondence, 1858–1871; CO 188: New Brunswick Original Correspondence, 1784–1867; CO 194: Newfoundland Original Correspondence, 1696–1922; CO 217: Nova Scotia and Cape Breton Original Correspondence, 1710–1867; CO 226: Prince Edward Island Original Correspondence, 1769–1873; CO 326, General Registers, 1633–1849; CO 327: British North America Emigration Registers, 1850–1863; CO 328: British North America General Registers (including emigration 1864–1868); CO 329: British North America Registers of Out-letters, 1872– 1880; PC 1: Privy Council and Privy Council Office: Miscellaneous Unbound Papers, 1481– 1946; PC 5: Privy Council Office: Plantation Books, 1678–1806; SP 54: Secretaries of State: State Papers Scotland Series II, 1688–1782 (for Scottish emigrants); and T 1: Treasury: Papers, 1557–1920.

Land grants
No systematic list or comprehensive index exists of the many varied land grants made in colonial America. C.M. Andrews in his *Guide to the Material for American History to 1783, in the Public Record Office of Great Britain* (Carnegie

Institution, 1912) gives references to the subject generally and to many individual grants. References to other grants can be obtained from the *Journals of the Board of Trade and Plantations*, the *Calendar of State Papers Colonial: America and West Indies*, and the *Acts of the Privy Council, Colonial Series*, all of which are available for consultation at the National Archives. Details of the grants referred to in the *Journals* can be found in the Colonial Office document class CO 5: America and West Indies, Original Correspondence. The records of many of the land grants made remained in the colonies and may be available in state archives.

Sources for 19th-century land grants can be found in CO 6: North American: Original Correspondence, 1816–1868, and CO 384: Original Correspondence, Emigration, 1817– 1896. Settlers in the 19th century, mainly British troops already stationed there, applied for land grants and CO 384/51 provides a list of North American settlers, giving personal details of age, career, marital status, children, purpose of application, and signature of applicant. This record covers the period 1837–8. Also, check records of the Land and Emigration Commission, which was established in 1833 to promote emigration; these contain records of free passages and land grants.

The Emigration Entry Books, 1814–1871 (CO 385) and the Land and Emigration Commission Papers, 1833–1894 (CO 386) give names of emigrants.

Hudson's Bay Company records
Founded in 1670, the Hudson's Bay Company's (HBC) chief interests for its first two centuries were the fur trade, exploration and settlement. After 1870, when its territory of Rupert's Land was incorporated into the Dominion of Canada, its interests became more varied.

BH 1 comprises the following eight types of records of the Hudson's Bay Company:
- headquarters records;
- records concerning posts in North America;
- logs, books and papers relating to ships in the service of the company;
- governors' papers;
- miscellaneous records, which include correspondence and journals of various individuals, as well as records of the Red River Settlement (1811–90), Vancouver Island colony (1848–61), Arctic expeditions (1824–66), and the parliamentary select committees;
- records of allied and subsidiary companies, which include the North West Company (1786–1851), the Puget's Sound Agricultural Company

(1838–1932), the International Financial Society Ltd (1859–69), the Russian American Company (1821–1903), the Assiniboine Wool Company (1829–36), the Red River Tallow Company (1832–3), the Vancouver Island Steam Sawmill Company (1852–6), the Vancouver Coal Mining Company (1861–1900) and the Buffalo Wool Company (1822–4);

- Western Department land records;
- records from the Commissioner's Office in Winnipeg.

The series also includes manuscript and published maps, charts and plans of Hudson's Bay Company forts, coal mines, various American and British territories and Canadian cities and towns, together with architects' drawings, specifications and atlases.

The records in BH 1 are microfilm copies of original records held at the Hudson's Bay Company Archives (HBCA). Further information about these records and the history of the company can be found at the HBCA website.

American Loyalist claims
The peace treaty signed at the end of the American War of Independence in 1783 provided for a recommendation by the Congress of the

United States for the restoration of the property of 'real British subjects'.

You can find records of the claims for compensation of American citizens who suffered property losses through loyalty to the British Crown during the American War of Independence in AO 12: Audit Office: American Loyalist Claims Series I, 1776–1812; AO 13: Audit Office: American Loyalist Claims Series II, 1780–1835; and T 79: American Loyalist Claims Commission, 1777–1841. These series consist of entry books and ledgers containing the evidence of witnesses, reports and other communicated documents, the examinations and decisions of the commissioners, lists of claims, etc.

An index to names in AO12 is available in the Research Enquiries Room at the National Archives. Next to the person's name is an abbreviation of the name of the state where the claimed loss occurred, followed by a volume number and a further number. The volume number gives you the reference to use when ordering the piece on the computer. For instance, in the entry Ackerly, Isaac, N.Y., V23, 21, V23 translates into piece 23, and AO 12/23 is the order reference. The second number, 21, is an internal reference and gives the page number in the volume on which the information can be found.

Rolls of declared accounts from the Auditors of the Imprest and the Commissioners of Audit relating to Loyalist claims can be found in AO 1. Papers concerning the claims and some compensation and pension lists of American loyalists and records of the Commissioners constituted to deal with the claims of loyalists and of British merchants under article 6 of the 1794 Treaty of Amity, Commerce and Navigation between Great Britain and the United States, and the convention between the two countries signed in 1802, can be found in Treasury records. T 50: Pay Lists and other Documents concerning Refugees, 1780–1856; and T 79: American Loyalist Claims Commission: Records, 1777–1841 contain the reports of commissioners investigating individual claims, and some compensation and pension lists.

You can find similar claims for compensation when East Florida was ceded to Spain in 1783 in T 77 for the period 1763–89. These include reports of the East Florida Claims Commission and lists of title deeds and papers relating to the management of estates. These consist primarily of the claims, with supporting documents, of the settlers of the province of East Florida, which, in 1783, after twenty years of British administration, was ceded to the Crown of Spain under article 5 of the Treaty of Paris. The claimants' papers, usually in the form of a memorial supported by documentation of land grants, indentures, schedules and valuations of property, and often with plans and other maps and plans, make up files 1–18. File 19 consists of reports on the claims of the many settlers who had taken refuge in the Bahamas. Unfortunately these records are not indexed by name of claimant.

Poor Law records
Many poor emigrants were provided with assistance for the passage by their parish, under the provisions of the 1834 Poor Law Amendment Act. The records of the administration of this assistance (MH 12) can include lists of emigrants, giving their occupation and destination; however, they are very voluminous and are arranged chronologically by county and Poor Law Union, not by subject, so you may find that details can be very difficult to find. Similar records relating to parish-organized emigration will be found locally at appropriate county record offices.

MH 19: Local Government Board and Predecessors: Correspondence with Government Offices, 1834–1909, contains correspondence of the Poor Law Commission and Board and the Local Government Board with other government departments, the Metropolitan Police, the

Metropolitan Board of Works and parliamentary officers relating to Poor Law administration and, after 1871, public health and local government services. MH 19/22 relates specifically to passage-assisted emigration and includes lists of emigrant ships reported to have arrived in British territories between 1836 and 1876.

Missionary records
The Fulham Papers in the Lambeth Palace Library comprise the archive of the bishops of London and date mainly from the 18th and 19th centuries. As well as covering the administration of the diocese of London, the archive contains correspondence on the other churches under the bishop's jurisdiction, notably those in America and the West Indies before the founding of the separate episcopates in those countries. The records also include ordination papers for the American and West Indies colonies, 1748–1824; lists of ministers receiving missionary bonds for the royal bounty for migration to the colonies, 1748–1811; appointments of clergy, 1718–74; lists of clergy and public officials, 1723–48; licences for curates, preachers, lecturers, schoolmasters, and licences to officiate in the colonies.

The library also holds returns of clergy queries. These were sent to all colonial clergy by

Bishop Edmund Gibson in 1723, and the returns present an interesting picture of colonial church life, with biographical information of the clergy.

Other papers available include those relating to emigration schemes and the assistance of those emigrating from the UK, 1905–28; Church Emigration Society papers; and an indexed calendar of the papers and correspondence of the Archbishop of Canterbury relating to Anglicans in the Antipodes, in particular emigration schemes, juvenile emigration and Empire settlement from the 1780s.

Other good sources for records relating to missionaries are the Church Mission Society, the Baptist Missionary Society and the School of Oriental and African Studies Library (Archives).

Passenger lists
Many outward passenger lists to North America have been published, particularly those that date before 1800 and relate to transportation. Some publications have been compiled from primary sources within the National Archives but most have been published using sources recording the arrival of emigrants in the destination countries. Check Chapter 6 for records relating to outward UK passenger lists to North America, including returns of births, marriages and deaths.

Female Emigration

TO

AUSTRALIA.

COMMITTEE:

EDWARD FORSTER, Esq. *Chairman.*
SAMUEL HOARE, Esq.
JOHN TAYLOR, Esq.
THOMAS LEWIN, Esq.

CHARLES HOLTE BRACEBRIDGE, Esq.
JOHN S. REYNOLDS, Esq.
JOHN PIRIE, Esq.
CAPEL CURE, Esq.
WILLIAM CRAWFORD, Esq.

CHARLES LUSHINGTON, Esq.
GEORGE LONG, Esq.
COLONEL PHIPPS,
NADIR BAXTER, Esq.
S. H. SHERRY, Esq.

The Committee for promoting the Emigration
OF

Single Women

To AUSTRALIA, under whose Management the Ships "Bussorah Merchant and Layton" were last Year despatched with Female Emigrants, acting under the Sanction His Majesty's Secretary of State for the Colonies, HEREBY GIVE NOTICE, That

A Fine SHIP of about 500 Tons Burthen,

Carrying an experienced Surgeon, and a respectable Person as Superintendent to secure the Comfort and Protection of the Emigrants during the Voyage, will sail from

GRAVESEND
On Thursday 1st of May next,
(Beyond which day she will on no account be detained) direct for

HOBART TOWN
VAN DIEMEN'S LAND.

Single Women and Widows of good Character, from 15 to 30 Years of Age, desirous of bettering their Condition by Emigrating to that healthy and highly prosperous Colony, where the number of Females compared with the entire Population is greatly deficient, and where consequently from the great demand for Servants, and other Female Employments, the Wages are comparatively high, may obtain a Passage

On payment of FIVE POUNDS only.

Those who are unable to raise that Sum here, will be allowed to give Notes of Hand, payable in the Colony within a reasonable time after their arrival, when they have acquired the means to do so, as they will have the advantage of the **Government Grant** in aid of their Passage.

The Females who proceed by this Conveyance will be taken care of on their first Landing at Hobart Town; they will find there a List of the various Situations to be obtained and of the Wages offered, and will be perfectly free to make their own Election; they will not be bound to any person, or subjected to any restraint, but will be, to all intents and purposes, perfectly free to act and decide for themselves.

Females in the Country who may desire to avail themselves of the important advantages thus offered them, should apply by Letter to "The Emigration Committee, London," under Cover addressed to "The UNDER SECRETARY OF STATE, COLONIAL DEPARTMENT, LONDON." It will be necessary that the Application be accompanied by a Certificate of Character from the Resident Minister of the Parish, or from some other respectable persons to whom the Applicant may be known; but the Certificate of Resident Minister is in all cases most desirable. Such Females as may find it expedient may, when approved by the Committee as fit persons to go by this Conveyance, boarded temporarily in London, prior to Embarkation, on Payment of 7s. per Week.

☞ All Applications made under cover in the foregoing manner, or personally, will receive early Answers, and all necessary Information, by applying to

JOHN MARSHALL, Agent to the Committee, 26, Birchin Lane, Cornhill.

EDWARD FORSTER, *Chairman.*

NOTE.—The Committee have the satisfaction to state that of 217 Females who went out by the Bussorah Merchant, 180 obtained good Situations within three Days of their Landing, and the remainder were all well placed within a few Days, under the advice of a Ladies' Committee, formed in the Colony expressly to aid the Females on their arrival.

LONDON, 22nd February, 1854.

By Authority:
PRINTED BY JOSEPH HARTNELL, FLEET STREET, FOR HIS MAJESTY'S STATIONERY OFFICE.

Chapter 8

Down under

- The realities of transportation
- Discovering the records: transportation
  Trial records
  Pardons, appeals and petitions
  Transportation lists
  Sources in Australia and New Zealand
- Discovering the records: free emigration
  Colonization of Australia and New Zealand
  Passenger lists
  Child migration schemes
  Sources in Australia and New Zealand

Unlike the early settlement of North America, the European settlement of Australia had a single motivating factor: making amends for one's criminal past. It began with the penal colony at Botany Bay on the east coast of Australia in 1787, and eventually in excess of 162,000 men, women and children were transported to Australia (New South Wales) and Tasmania (then called Van Diemen's Land) between 1787 and 1867.

The realities of transportation

Transportation of convicts was not a matter of simply dumping human refuse on the colonies: the aim was for the convict to be forced to learn good work habits of industry and self-discipline, while at the same time benefiting the development of the colonial economy. Usually it was the young who were transported: after all, they were the most likely to benefit from a new life in a new world, and the most likely to be fit enough to supply the necessary productive labour. As a system it was genuinely thought by the home government to be effective, efficient and humane. The colonial authorities, not unnaturally, tended to take a more jaundiced view of the benefits of transportation, and bitterly resented it.

An order by the Privy Council in 1615 resulted in it becoming increasingly common for a death sentence to be remitted, on a pardon, to transportation overseas. In 1718 an Act of Parliament (4 Geo. I, c. 11) standardized transportation to America at 14 years for those who had been sentenced to death and introduced a new penalty – transportation for 7 years – as a sentence in its own right for a range of non-capital offences. Between 1614 and 1775, more than 50,000 men, women and children were dispatched from the British Isles to the English colonies in North America.

Although transportation ceased with the outbreak of the American War of Independence (American Revolution) in 1776, sentences of transportation were still passed. The prisons rapidly became overcrowded, overflowing into old ships ('hulks') moored in coastal waters. The solution was to develop a new penal colony, and in 1787 the First Fleet of eleven ships set sail for Botany Bay on the east coast of Australia. A second fleet followed in 1790 and a third left in 1791. Transportation to Tasmania (Van Diemen's Land) began in 1803.

Estimates suggest that over 1,000 ships transported those 162,000 men, women and children to Australasia between 1787 and 1867. In the 1830s, 4,000 people were being transported every year, with a further 9,500 male convicts transported to Western Australia from 1850 to 1868.

In 1857 transportation was effectively abolished, though the Home Secretary retained the right to impose transportation for specific offences until 1868.

Australia also attracted free settlers through the Colonial Office, as did New Zealand, which was not used as a penal colony.

Discovering the records: transportation

Trial records

You can find surviving records of court of assize trials at the National Archives. The assize judges mainly dealt with the more serious criminal offences not normally handled by the local courts of Quarter Sessions. Offences dealt with ranged from murder, infanticide, theft (stolen goods were often undervalued as worth less than 12d to avoid making it a capital offence), highway robbery, rape, assault, coining, forgery and witchcraft, to trespass, vagrancy and recusancy. The assize records are not indexed by personal name: instead, they are arranged by assize circuit, and then by record type. To find a particular case, you must know the name of accused; the county or circuit where he or she was tried and the approximate date of the trial. For the 19th century, if you do not know where or when the accused was tried, you can look at the Annual Criminal Registers, for England and Wales, 1805–92, in HO 27, or in HO 26, Criminal Registers, for Middlesex, 1791–1849. Available on microfiche in the Microfilm Reading Room is an index to HO 27, arranged by county and then by name within, though these records are in the process of being digitized to be made available online.

Both series list those charged with indictable offences, giving place of trial, verdict and sentence. Once a reference to a date and place of trial has been established, it is then possible to check the various series of records for criminal assizes held in English and Welsh assizes. Survival of assize records is patchy, as the clerks of assize, who kept them, tended to destroy them when their bulk became too much. If a suitable record exists for the year and place in question, this will be identified on the National Archives online catalogue. Records of trials at courts of Quarter Sessions are *not* in the National Archives, but at local record offices.

The best place to begin a search in the assize

records themselves is with the Crown Minute Book, Gaol Book or Agenda Book if one survives – these list the accused and summarize cases heard or about to be heard, often noting the plea, verdict and sentence. The indictments are the formal statement of the charge against the accused, usually annotated with plea, verdict and sentence, and filed in large unwieldy bundles together with other miscellaneous records such as jury panels, coroner's inquests, commissions and presentments of non-criminal offences. Depositions and Examinations can be full of personal details but have mostly not survived. Transcripts of proceedings or shorthand notes of what was actually said in court do not normally survive, although contemporary newspapers or pamphlets often reported local cases in much detail. Local newspapers may be consulted at the British Library's Newspaper Library, or some-times at the appropriate local county record office or library.

London and Middlesex sessions before 1834 were held before the lord mayor acting as chief justice together with other commissioners acting as judges. In practice most cases were held by legal officers, notably the Recorder and Common Serjeant of London. Records of Guildhall Sessions, relating to the City, are held by the

Corporation of London Record Office, Guildhall. Records of Old Bailey sessions for the rest of London and Middlesex are at the London Metropolitan Archives.

The Central Criminal Court was established in 1834 by the Central Criminal Court Act (4 & 5 Will. V, c. 36) and empowered to try treasons, murders, felonies and misdemeanours committed in London and Middlesex and certain parts of Essex, Kent and Surrey. The records of the Central Criminal Court are arranged chronologically and are not indexed by personal name – you must have an approximate date of trial to begin a search.

Printed proceedings or narrative accounts of trials for London and Middlesex sessions for 1801–1904 are at the National Archives in the series PCOM 1. Old Bailey proceedings 1714–1834 are also available on microfilm. Duplicates of these volumes are also in CRIM 10 covering the period 1834–1912 and provide a detailed record of minutes of evidence for many of the trials. Those for 1714–1834 are now available online in a fully searchable format at the Old Bailey website. They were not kept after 1912 but contemporary newspaper reports often record proceedings in great detail and may be consulted at the British Library's Newspaper Library in

Colindale. British Trials 1660–1900 (it includes a few trials 1901–8) is available on microfilm and includes additional contemporary pamphlet accounts of trials as well as reproducing many of the Old Bailey proceedings. There are separate indexes, including by name of defendant.

Pardons, appeals and petitions
Applications for clemency are often an excellent source of personal information. Anyone asking for clemency or a pardon would be anxious to prove that they were worthy of mercy, and to show how respectable they were they would offer just the kind of details about personal circumstances and family background that family historians want to know. The National Archives holds a range of these documents.

HO 17: Criminal Petitions, Series I, 1819–1839 and HO 18: Home Office: Criminal Petitions, Series II, 1839–1854 are arranged in coded bundles so you will need to use the registers in HO 19 to identify the right one. These are arranged by the date of receipt of the petition, beginning in 1797. Since they include information about the response to the petition, you can sometimes find out something useful about a convict even if the petition itself does not survive.

There are also petitions in HO 48: Law Officers' Reports, Opinions and Correspondence, 1782–1871; HO 49: Law Officers' Letter Books, 1762–1871; HO 54: Civil Petitions and Addresses, 1783–1854; and HO 56: Petitions Entry Books, 1784–1922. These records, however, are not indexed.

HO 47: Judges' Reports on Criminals, 1784–1829, and HO 6: Judges' and Recorders' Returns, 1816–1840, are also informative. They sometimes include an unofficial transcript of evidence (together with comments on the characters of both witnesses and juries) as well as memorials and petitions from friends and relatives of the accused. The *Calendars of Home Office Papers, George III, 1760–1775*, also include judges' reports on criminals. HO 47 is now searchable by name of convict, place and year of trial and details of crime, including names of victims where appropriate, in the National Archives online catalogue.

It was possible for wives to accompany their convict husbands, and some wives applied to do so. Their petitions survive in PC 1: Privy Council and Privy Council Office: Miscellaneous Unbound Papers, notably PC 1/67–92 for 1819–44, and from 1849 to 1871 in HO 12: Criminal Department: Old Criminal (OC) Papers. HO 12 references can be identified via HO 14: Criminal Department: Registers of Papers, 1849–1870. CO 201: New South Wales Original Correspondence, 1783–1900, and CO 386: Colonial Office: Land and Emigration Commission, etc., 1833–1894, include letters from people wishing to join convict relatives. For example. CO 386/154 consists of a register of applications for passages to the colonies for convicts' families, 1848–73.

Transportation lists
HO 11: Convict Transportation, 1787–1870, provides the name of the ship on which the convict sailed as well as the date and place of conviction and the term of the sentence. They are not indexed by name of convict, but if you know the name of the ship and preferably also when it either left England or arrived in Australia, it should be relatively easy to find the convict. There is a card index to convict ships in the Research Enquiries Room at Kew. It refers to records in HO 11 and ADM 101: Office of the Director General of the Medical Department of the Navy and predecessors: Medical Journals, 1785–1963. ADM 101 includes journals from convict ships and emigrant ships, for which naval surgeons were provided. The journals contain an account of the treatment of medical and surgical cases, and

usually a copy of the daily sick list, statistical abstracts of the incidence of diseases, and general comments on the health and activities of the ship's company. Similar journals can be found in MT 32: Admiralty Transport Department, Surgeon Superintendents' Journals of Convict Ships, 1858–1867.

PC 1: Privy Council and Privy Council Office: Miscellaneous Unbound Papers, 1481–1946, and PC 2: Privy Council: Registers, 1540–1978, contain additional material about transportation. The registers, for example, give lists of convicts transported for 14 years or less. TS 18: Treasury Solicitor: General Series Papers, 1517–1923, includes contracts with agents to transport the prisoners, with full lists of ships and convicts, 1842–67, in TS 18/460–525 and 1308–1361. Reports on the medical condition of the convicts while at sea may be found in the Admiralty medical journals, 1817–56 (ADM 101), and in the Admiralty Transport Department surgeon-superintendents' journals, 1858–67 (MT 32).

Records of those awaiting transportation in prison hulks (ship prisons) are also available at the National Archives. HO 8: Home Office: Convict Prisons: Quarterly Returns of Prisoners, 1824–1876, consists of sworn lists of convicts on board the hulks and in convict prisons with particulars as to their ages, convictions and sentences, health and behaviour.

Sources in Australia and New Zealand
There is no single index to the names of those transported to Australia. In order to find out more about a convict you will need to have a good idea of when they were tried and/or the date of transportation and ship in which they sailed to Australia.

Details of convicts who sailed on the early fleets have been published in books such as Fidlon & Ryan's *The First Fleeters* (1981). For later years, names of convicts and settlers appear on the published censuses for the penal colonies, the most complete being the census of New South Wales in November 1828. Edited by M.R. Sainty and K.A. Johnson, this census was published in 1980 by the Library of Australian History. The original records of the 1828 census are available on microfilm at the National Archives in the series HO 10.

Details of convicts may also be found on the microfiche index to the New South Wales Convict Indents and Ships. Compiled by the Genealogical Society of Victoria, the index records the names and aliases of some 150,000 convicts who arrived in New South Wales and Van Diemen's

Land between 1788 and 1842, when transportation to New South Wales effectively ended.
The index is almost wholly based on the Ships'
Indents (Indentures) which are the documents
recording the formal transfer of prisoners to the
governor of the colony receiving them. Each
entry in the index (available in the Microfilm
Reading Room) records the name or alias of the
convict, the name of the ship and its arrival date,
and a reference to the relevant page(s) on the
Indent(s) that have been reproduced on microfiche by State Records New South Wales as part
of their Genealogical Research Kit. The fiche
collection also includes an index of ships that
transported the convicts. It shows the arrival date
for each voyage, together with the particular fiche
and film that contains the records. A CD-ROM
version of these indexes is available in the
National Archives Library.

   All the above sources are available at the
National Archives and the Society of Genealogists.

   The Genealogical Society of Victoria also has
catalogues relating to the 80,000 convicts transported to New South Wales between 1788 and
1849, the 70,000 bound for Tasmania (1803–53)
and 10,000 male convicts transported to Western
Australia (1850–3). Catalogues include records

relating to convict arrivals, musters and papers, assignment registers, registers of tickets of leave, registers of pardons, applications for marriage, and convict death returns. The records here also provide details of convicts' children in Tasmania, many of whom arrived with their convict parent or parents and were unnamed on the convict lists. The records comprise information relating to destitute children and refer to the setting up of an orphanage by Governor Arthur, in 1825, to house the many destitute children.

Discovering the records: free emigration

Colonization of Australia and New Zealand
The records of the Colonial Office at the National Archives include much material relating to free emigrants to all colonies. In CO 384: Emigration Original Correspondence, 1817–1896, you can find many letters from settlers or people intending to settle in the colonies. Details of land grants and applications may be found in CO 323: Colonies, General: Original Correspondence, 1689–1952; CO 324: Colonies, General: Entry Books Series I, 1662–1872; and CO 381: Colonies, General: Entry Books Series II, 1835–1872.

The Land and Emigration Commission was

established in 1833 to promote emigration by providing free passage and land grants. The Emigration Entry Books, 1814–71 (CO 385) and the Land and Emigration Commission Papers, 1833–94 (CO 386) give names of emigrants. CO 386 also contains records of the South Australian Colonization Commission, a predecessor of the Land and Emigration Commission, responsible for laying down the regulations for land sales and overseeing the selection of emigrants eligible for a free passage. In the document CO 386/29 you can find details of the government regulations set for local agents when selecting emigrants for free passages to New South Wales, Western Australia, Tasmania and New Zealand. The criteria for selection were very strict. You can often find references to payments which covered emigrants' travel expenses to their port of embarkation in locally kept parish records. Other general Colonial Office sources for emigrants include individual colony's entry books, government gazettes, blue books and colonial newspapers.

AUSTRALIA
CO 386/21 gives the regulations governing the colonization of Australia through the Wakefield Scheme of 1829, whereby land was sold for a

substantial price in the colony and the funds thus generated used to ship emigrant labourers from Britain to work the land. Those purchasing the land were assured of an adequate supply of labour of the right type, since labourers were vetted before being given the passage. The labourer was promised a new and more prosperous life in a colony where labour was in demand, while prospects were poor at home. The scheme proposed to set up a colony along approved lines and at the same time relieve unemployment and pauperism at home.

The South Australian Colonization Commission, a predecessor of the Land and Emigration Commission, was responsible for laying down the regulations for land sales and overseeing the selection of emigrants eligible for a free passage.

The documents CO 386/142–143, 145–146, and 148–152 contain information relating to the Wakefield scheme, the South Australian Colonization Commission, the sale of land in Australia to individuals, and labourers' applications for free passages.

Some of the better family history sources can be found in CO 201: New South Wales Original Correspondence, 1783–1900, which includes lists of settlers, 1801–21. The correspondence of 1823 to 1833 has also been indexed in a supplementary finding aid to this series, available in the Research Enquiries Room at the National Archives. CO 386: Land and Emigration Commission, etc., 1833–1894, contains original correspondence and entry books of the Agent General for Emigration, the South Australian Commissioners and the Land and Emigration Commission.

Furthermore, you can find names of Australian settlers in CO 202: New South Wales Entry Books, 1786–1873; CO 360: New South Wales Register of Correspondence, 1849–1900; and CO 368: New South Wales Register of Out-Letters, 1873–1900. Similarly, names of New Zealand settlers can be traced in CO 209: New Zealand Original Correspondence, 1830–1922.

The censuses of New South Wales and Tasmania conducted at intervals between 1788 and 1859 are valuable sources. Although primarily conducted to record convict details, you will find that the censuses do include the names of individuals who 'came free' or who were 'born in the colony'.

NEW ZEALAND

Unlike Australia, New Zealand was not used as a penal colony. You can find details of emigrants to New Zealand in CO 208: New Zealand Company

Original Correspondence, 1839–1858. The New Zealand Company was formed in 1839 and incorporated in 1841 with power to buy, sell, settle and cultivate land in New Zealand. It surrendered its charter in 1850 and was dissolved in 1858. This series of records contains registers of cabin passengers emigrating, 1839–50, in CO 208/269–272; applications for free passage, 1839–50, in CO 208/273–274 (indexed in CO 208/275); applications for land, lists of land-owners, in CO 208/254–255; lists of agents and surveyors, lists of German emigrants and lists of maintained emigrants in CO 208/278–281.

Between 1846 and 1851, army pensioners were encouraged to settle in New South Wales and New Zealand, although many of them failed as settlers. WO 43: War Office: Secretary-at-War, Correspondence, Very Old Series (VOS) and Old Series (OS), 1809–1857, contain papers relating to particular emigrant officers and soldiers in relation to half-pay, pensions, annuities and allowances. Similarly, references to former soldiers who settled in any colony can be found in WO 22: Royal Hospital Chelsea: Pensions Returns, 1842–1883.

You can also find reference to ex-soldier emigrants to Australia, 1830–48, in WO 43/542. Similarly, WO 43/543 relates to New Zealand

Spotlight: The Bee Gees

Barry Gibb (born 1946) and his younger twin brothers Robin (born 1949) and Maurice (1949–2003) emigrated to Redcliffe, Queensland, Australia with their parents Harold and Barbara, older sister Lesley and younger brother Andy in August 1958, aboard the SS *Fairsea*. The entry on the passenger list at the National Archives (BT 27/1851) shows that Harold was a 'Collector Salesman' and that they had lived at 71 Northern Grove, Didsbury, near Manchester. The family migrated as part of the New Life emigration scheme, also known as the '£10 Pom'.

By 1960 The Bee Gees – the musical trio formed by Barry and the twins – were featured on television shows, and they started releasing singles three years later. The family decided to return to the UK in 1966. En route home they discovered that The Bee Gees' hit 'Spicks and Specks' had reached Number 1 in the Australian singles chart, the beginning of a commercially successful career that would span over 30 years.

returns. Pension return records for District Offices survive for New South Wales, 1849–80 in WO 22/272–275; for South Australia, Queensland, Tasmania and Victoria, 1876–80 in WO 22/227, 297, 298 and 300; and for New

Zealand, 1845–54 and 1875–80 in WO 22/
276–293.

Passenger lists
Many outward passenger lists to Australasia have
been published, particularly those that date
before 1800 and relate to transportation. Some
publications have been compiled from primary
sources within the National Archives but most
have been published using sources recording the
arrival of emigrants in the destination countries.
Check Chapter 6 for records relating to outward
UK passenger lists to Australasia, including
returns of births, marriages and deaths on board
vessels bound for Australasia, and available
printed and online sources

Child migration schemes
For information and sources relating to various
British child emigration schemes that operated
from 1618 to 1967 migrating some 150,000
children from the UK to the British Colonies and
Dominions, *see* Chapter 10.

Sources in Australia and New Zealand
The National Archives of Australia website holds
an abundance of material on British emigrants. It
has free Research Guides, available to download,

on various 20th-century British migration schemes, including selected documents for British people who migrated to Australia under the assisted passage schemes after 1950, known as the '£10 Pom' scheme.

Similarly, the Archives New Zealand website holds information relating to British migrants.

Unfortunately, there are no available 20th-century census returns for you to check for British migrants. Censuses have been held in Australia in 1901, 1911, 1921, 1933, 1947, 1954, 1966, 1971, 1976, 1981, 1986, 1991 and 1996, but each has been destroyed after statistical extractions have been made. However, the census taken in August 2001 provided for returns to be retained providing those completing the returns requested it, although the retained returns will not be available to public inspection for 100 years. A similar picture exists for New Zealand.

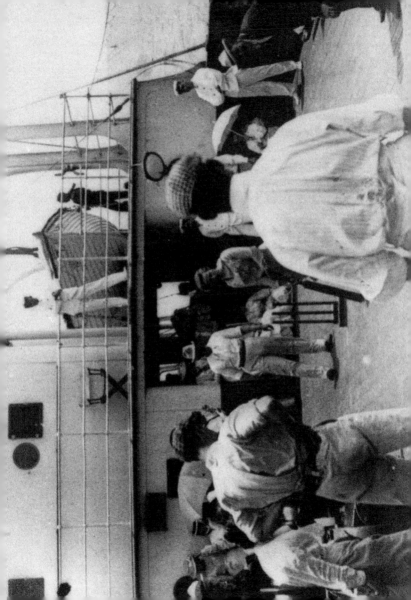

Chapter 9

Further afield

- Africa
- The Indian sub-continent
- The Middle East
- South America
- Discovering the records
  General sources and printed material
  Missionary records
  Emigrating to South Africa
  Emigrating to India
  Emigrating to Patagonia
  Emigrating to the Middle East

As new lands were discovered and trade routes established, many people were enticed abroad by the promise of riches. By the end of the 18th century around 1.7 million people had left the UK to seek their fortunes in the colonies, and this number swelled by a further 10 million during the 19th and 20th centuries. Although the bulk of migrants went to North America and Australasia, a significant number went to other colonies.

Africa

In Africa, the Cape of Good Hope formally became a British colony in 1814, followed by Natal in 1843 and, by 1902, the former Boer republics of the Orange Free State and Transvaal. In 1910 Cape Colony, Orange River Colony, Natal and Transvaal united to form the new Union of South Africa. All provinces attracted British settlers.

The Indian sub-continent

The Indian sub-continent also attracted a large number of migrants. The East India Company, established in 1600 as a joint-stock association of English merchants, established a network of warehouses or 'factories' throughout south and east Asia. Over a period of 250 years it underwent several substantial changes in its basic character and functions, becoming, during the second half of the 18th century, a major territorial power in India with its headquarters in Calcutta. The political implications of this development eventually caused the British government in 1784 to institute standing Commissioners (the Board of Control) in London to exercise supervision over the Company's Indian policies, and subsequently led to the Acts of Parliament of 1813 and 1833 which opened British trade with the East Indies to all shipping and resulted in the Company's complete withdrawal from its commercial functions. The Company continued to exercise responsibility, under the supervision of the Board, for the government of India until the India Act of 1858.

With the India Act, the Company and the Board of Control were replaced by a single new department of state, the India Office, which functioned, under the Secretary of State for India, as an executive office of United Kingdom government alongside the Foreign Office, Colonial Office, Home Office and War Office. The Secretary of State for India inherited all the executive functions previously carried out by the Company, and all the powers of 'superintendence, direction and control' over the British government in India previously exercised by the Board of Control. Improved communications with India – the overland and submarine telegraph cables (1868–70) and the opening of the Suez Canal (1869) – rendered this control, exercised through the viceroy and provincial governors, more effective in the last quarter of the 19th century. It was only with the constitutional reforms initiated during the First World War, and carried forward by the India Acts of 1919 and 1935, that there came about a significant relaxation of India Office supervision over the government of India and with it, in India, a gradual devolution of authority to legislative bodies and local governments. The same administrative reforms also led in 1937 to the separation of Burma from India and the creation in London of the Burma Office, separate from the India Office though sharing the same Secretary of State and located in the same building. With the grant of independence to India and Pakistan in 1947, and to Burma in 1948, both the India Office and the Burma Office were dissolved.

The Middle East

The Middle East was the destination for some emigrants. The Levant Company was established

---

Spotlight: Cliff Richard and Spike Milligan

The British Library Asia, Pacific & Africa Collections hold extensive records relating to colonial life in India, including an expanding biographical card index with details of some 295,000 civil and military personnel, their families and others.

Many famous British faces were born in India and other parts of the Commonwealth to civil and military personnel. They include Terence Alan (aka Spike) Milligan, comedian, Goon, and author, who was born on 16 April 1918 in Ahmednagar, near Bombay, India, when the country was still the jewel in the crown of the British Empire. His father, Leo Alphonso Milligan was a soldier.

Britain's most successful solo recording artist, Cliff Richard (real name Harry Webb) was born in Lucknow, India, on 14 October 1940. His father, Roger Webb, had moved to India to help build the railways.

Both men appear in the passenger lists at the National Archives.

---

in 1581 when its members were granted a monopoly of English trade with the Turkish Empire. Its representative at the Turkish court at Constantinople was also given diplomatic authority as English ambassador.

Subsequently, consulates, which were

manned by representatives of the Levant Company, were appointed at strategic trading posts throughout the western Turkish Empire, including Aleppo, Algiers, Cairo, Chios, Patras, Salonika, Smyrna, Tunis and Zante.

By the second half of the 18th century, the Levant Company was in financial difficulties and could no longer afford to maintain the ambassador and consuls without government subsidy.

In 1804, the Foreign Office took over full responsibility for the British embassy at Constantinople and the Company appointed its own consul general to look after its commercial interests. The consuls had enforced the ordinances of the company throughout the Levant, levied consulage on imports and exports, maintained law and order, adjudicated disputes, administered the estates of Englishmen who died abroad, and exercised control over the factors who were the local representatives of merchants based in London. Large factories, such as Aleppo, also appointed a salaried treasurer and a chancellor, who recorded all the official business of the factory and registered all acts, contracts and wills made by the factors.

South America

South America, too, attracted British migrants. In 1865 a Welsh-speaking colony, called in Welsh Y Wladfa ('The Colony'), was established in the valley of the Chubut River in Patagonia in Argentina. The original emigrants sailed from Liverpool on the *Mimosa*. In the 1880s a further colony was established in the foothills of the Andes and this was called Cwm Hyfryd ('Pleasant Valley'). Although measures were later taken to remove some of the colonists to Canada and South Africa, most of the settlers and their descendants remained in Argentina.

Discovering the records

General sources and printed material
You will find that much of the information relating to emigration to the colonies has been printed in some form. Most of it is administrative in character, but it can include useful genealogical material. Main published sources include the records of the National Archives, specifically Privy Council (PC 1, PC 2 and PC 5), printed as *Acts of the Privy Council of England, Colonial Series*. Various useful classes of Treasury papers, registers and indexes including T 1, T 2, T 3, T 4 and

T 108, contain considerable reference to Colonial Office business. Many of these have been described and indexed in the *Calendar of Treasury Papers, 1557 to 1728*, the *Calendar of Treasury Books, 1660–1718* and the *Calendar of Treasury Books and Papers, 1729 to 1745*, and include reference to other Treasury series, such as T 7: Treasury: Books of Out-letters concerning Colonial Affairs, 1849–1921; T 27: General Out-letter Books, 1668–1920; T 28: Treasury: Various Out-letter Books, 1763–1885; T 29: Minute Books, 1667–1870; T 38: Treasury: Departmental Accounts, 1558–1937; and T 99: Minute Books, Supplementary, 1690–1832; T 52: Entry Books of Royal Warrants, 1667–1857; T 53: Entry Books of Royal Warrants Relating to the Payment of Money, 1676–1839; T 54: Entry Books of Warrants concerning Appointments, Crown Leases and other, 1667 to 1849; and T 60: Order Books, 1667–1831.

Many senior civil servants who were posted for service overseas or in the colonies are best sought, not in the records, but in such publications as the *Dictionary of National Biography*, or the *British Biographical Archive*. There are a number of official printed sources available at Kew on the postings of senior civil servants, but they do not provide personal information. The main one is the *British Imperial Calendar*, which runs from 1810 to 1972, when it became the *Civil Service Year Book*. From 1852 there is the *Foreign Office List*, and from 1862 the *Colonial Office List*. The *Diplomatic Service List* runs from 1966, and the *Commonwealth Relations Office List* from 1953. All are available at the National Archives, as is another useful source: David P. Henige, *Colonial Governors from the Fifteenth Century to the Present: A Comprehensive List* (Madison: University of Wisconsin Press, 1970).

The records of the Colonial Office include much material relating to emigrants to all colonies. CO 384: Emigration Original Correspondence, 1817–1896, contains many letters from settlers or people intending to settle in British colonies. Other general Colonial Office sources for emigrants include individual colony's entry books, government gazettes, blue books and colonial newspapers.

Entry books (available to the late 19th century for most colonies) you will find particularly useful, as they can include details of patents and grants of land. Colonial government gazettes and colonial newspapers are similar in style and in the type of information they provide. As well as statistical information on subjects such as population, geography and accounts, they also contain a wealth of information of interest to genealogists. These include:

- birth, marriage and death notifications (and occasionally obituaries);
- notices of proceedings and sales in the local courts of Chancery and Petty Sessions;
- lists of people applying for liquor licenses, dog licenses, gun licences, etc.;
- lists of jurors, constables, nurses, druggists, solicitors, etc.;
- notices of sales of land, public appointments, leave of absence and resumption of duty;
- notices relating to cases of intestacy, wills, executors, etc.;
- notices on applications for naturalization;
- inquests into wrecks;
- lists of ships entering and clearing port, often with the names of first-class passengers;
- lists of people in arrears of militia tax;
- lists of people who paid parish relief.

The recording of appointments and promotions can also help to piece together the careers of colonial civil servants. References to individual colony series of government gazettes and colonial newspapers can be found on the online catalogue and also in A. Thurston, *Records of the Colonial Office, Dominions Office, Common-*

wealth Relations Office and Commonwealth Office (London: PRO, 1995). The British Library Newspaper Library also holds an excellent collection of colonial newspapers and early gazettes.

Missionary records

There are a number of collections of missionary society records which may assist in the tracing of emigrants. Most of these are discussed in Chapter 7, as many schemes related to North America, but the following archives hold rich sources relating to missionaries: Lambeth Palace Library; the Church Mission Society; the Baptist Missionary Society; the School of Oriental and African Studies (SOAS).

A major SOAS collection comprises the Missionary Archives, including those of the China Inland Mission (now the Overseas Missionary Fellowship), 1872–1951; the Conference of British Missionary Societies, 1910–12; the London Missionary Society (now the Council for World Mission), 1795–1970; the Melanesian Mission, c.1872–1970; the Presbyterian Church of England's Foreign Missions Committee.

Founded in 1799, the Church Mission Society (CMS) was established to send Christians, lay and clergy, to Africa and the East to share the 'Good News' proclaimed by Jesus Christ.

With an estimated 2,000,000 items, the Special Collections section of the University of Birmingham library holds by far the largest collection of CMS archives. This has been received in instalments from 1979, and papers from the Society's foundation in 1799 up to 1949 are currently open for scholarly study. The collection is a rich source of information, not only for ecclesiastical history and missiology, but for the secular history and anthropology of the many countries, particularly in Asia and Africa, in which the Society has operated. Included are records of the Society's home administration (minute books, ledgers, correspondence and publications) and of the work of individual missions, amongst them letters and diaries kept by missionaries. Over the years the Society has absorbed three other missionary societies, and their archives too now form part of the collection in the university library; they are the Church of England Zenana Missionary Society (founded 1880), the Female Education Society (founded 1834) and the Loochoo Naval Mission (founded 1843).

The Baptist Missionary Society (BMS), founded by William Carey when he set out for India in 1793, has deposited its archives at Regent's Park College, Oxford. The archives there include missionary correspondence.

Emigrating to South Africa
If your ancestors migrated to South Africa, Colonial Office records at the National Archives may assist you with your research. CO 48: Cape of Good Hope Colony (Cape Colony), Original Correspondence, 1807–1910, contains letters from settlers and papers about grants of land at the Cape of Good Hope, 1814–25. For the same colony, there are CO 49: Cape of Good Hope Colony (Cape Colony), Entry Books, 1795–1872; CO 336: Cape of Good Hope (Cape Colony) Register of Correspondence, 1850–1910; and CO 462: Cape of Good Hope (Cape Colony) Register of Out-letters, 1872–1910. All the series contain references to individual settlers. WO 148: Civilian Claims to Military Compensation Boards, South African War, 1900–1905, contains a representative selection of registers, indexes and files relating to claims made by civilians to the Central and District Military Compensation Boards in respect of losses suffered by reason of the South African war, or for property requisitioned by the military forces.

Registers of payments to army and navy pensioners (including some widows and orphans) at the Cape of Good Hope and elsewhere in South Africa, 1849–58 and 1876–80, are in WO 22/243–244. The muster rolls of the Cape

Levies, 1851–3, may prove useful (WO 13/3718–3725).

There are two excellent published works relating to British settlers in South Africa: P. Philip, *British Residents at the Cape, 1795–1819* and E. Bull, *Aided Immigration from Britain to South Africa*. Both have compiled lists of settlers using original sources and provide information relating to particular 19th-century emigration schemes, such as the Byrne Settlers who came from all over the UK to Natal.

For settlers after 1910, when South Africa became the Union of South Africa, individual files on immigrants are available via the Department of Home Affairs in South Africa, or check the National Archives of South Africa website.

Emigrating to India

THE BRITISH LIBRARY RECORDS

The British Library, Asia, Pacific and Africa Collections (formerly Oriental and India Office Collections), holds records relating to the British administration of India prior to independence in 1947.

The records comprise the archives of the East India Company (1600–1858), of the Board of Control or Board of Commissioners for the Affairs of India (1784–1858), of the India Office (1858–1947), of the Burma Office (1937–48) and of a number of related British agencies overseas. The India Office Records are administered by the British Library as part of the public records of the United Kingdom, and are open for public consultation under the provisions of the Public Record Acts and in accordance with regulations established by the Lord Chancellor.

The Asia, Pacific and Africa Collections contain extensive records of India for both the period 1600 to 1858, when the East India Company controlled the region, and that from 1858 to 1947, when India was ruled by the British government through the India Office. Among the numerous sources there is a card index with details of nearly 300,000 civil and military personnel, their families and others. The collections also contain registers of births, marriages and burials arranged by presidency (Bengal, Bombay, Madras), registered wills of the three presidencies, railway employees, and service records for military personnel in the East India Company and the Indian Army.

The National Archives holds a run of the annual *East India Register*, continued by the *India List* (under various titles) from 1791 to 1947, as well as the separate *Indian Army List*. The Asia,

Pacific and Africa Collections also hold an incomplete series of writers' petitions 1749–1856, and appointment papers for East India Company civil servants with baptismal certificates and educational testimonials. Brief service records for high-ranking civil servants appear in the *India Office List* 1886–1947. Histories of service (V/12 series) for higher-ranking officers from 1879 give promotions and postings, sometimes dates of birth. Civil lists (V/13 series) for lower-rank officials from 1840 do not give a continuous career record, and searchers consequently need to consult a sequence of annual volumes to establish an individual's career.

Records of personnel employed in government railways, police, public works, post office, etc., 1818–1900 and 1922–8, can be found in L/F/10 series. Name, occupation, salary and period of residence in India is usually provided in these records. Deaths in the Uncovenanted Civil Service 1870–1949 are found in L/AG/34/14A. These records give name of deceased, date and place of death, rank, age, native town and country, next of kin, custody of property if any. There is a separate card index in the Reading Room at Kew. Also available are records of appointments in the United Kingdom to employment in Indian railway companies 1848–1925: L/AG/46/4, L/AG/46/10–12 and L/AG/46/18 series. Again, for these records you need to access the separate nominal card index in the Reading Room. Finally, there are also personal records relating to the Queen's India Cadetships 1858–1930: L/MIL/9/292–302; Sandhurst cadets commissioned into the Indian Army Unattached List 1859–1940: L/MIL/9/ 303–319; Quetta cadets 1915–18: L/MIL/9/320–332; and assistant surgeons' and surgeons' papers 1804–914: L/MIL/ 9/358–408.

For records of service for officers, surgeons, departmental warrant officers, NCOs and privates, see I.A. Baxter, *India Office Library and Records: A Brief Guide to Biographical Sources*. For officers of the Bengal Army 1758–1834, see V.C.P. Hodson, *List of the Officers of the Bengal Army* (4 vols, London, 1927–47). For surgeons, see D.G. Crawford, *Roll of the Indian Medical Service 1615–1930* (London, 1930).

Also, the European Manuscripts collection of the British Library houses the private papers of several hundred people who served in India, including viceroys and governors, civil servants, army officers and other ranks, businessmen, missionaries, scholars, travellers and their families. This growing collection (now over 16,000 volumes) of letters, diaries, papers of all kinds and tape-recordings supplements the official records and illustrates the wide diversity of work and social life in India and neighbouring countries since 1650.

OTHER SOURCES
Although the British Library Asia, Pacific and Africa Collections is the main source for tracing migrants to India, you can find other useful information elsewhere. The Society of Genealogists has an excellent collection of material relating to emigration to India, including birth, marriage and death announcements (and obituaries), extracted from Indian newspapers.

The National Archives holds the series of records FO 41: General Correspondence before 1906, East India Company, 1776–1797, which consists of correspondence with the Court of Directors of the East India Company. Also check CO 77: East Indies Original Correspondence, Entry Books, 1570–1856. This series contains original correspondence and entry relating to the East Indies and includes documents relating to Persia (now Iran) and China, and to the embassy to China of 1793 to 1794.

The *Calendar of State Papers East Indies, 1513–1668* (five volumes) calendars material available at both the British Library and the National Archives.

Emigrating to Patagonia
The National Archives holds a wealth of information relating to the Welsh-speaking colony of Patagonia. Try searching the online catalogue using the terms 'Patagonia', 'Chubut' and 'Chupat'; you will find various sources, including ADM (Admiralty), FO (Foreign Office), HO (Home Office) and SP (State Papers Department). Details of the earlier settlers can be found on surviving crew lists and official logs of the *Mimosa*, the tea-clipper which landed in New Bay (Port Madryn) on 28 July 1865 with the first 150 settlers.

Emigrating to the Middle East
You can find records of the Levant Company at the National Archives. SP 105: Secretaries of State: State Papers Foreign, Archives of British Legations, 1568–1871, consists of letter books and correspondence of British embassies and legations abroad mainly to the year 1796. The series includes records of the Levant Company's London-based governing body, the General Court, and its officers, including minute books of the General Court (1611 to 1706), letter books of instructions to ambassadors, consuls and other agents (1606 to 1825), and treasurer's accounts. Of the Company's diplomatic and consular

missions, only Constantinople, Aleppo, Smyrna and Cairo are represented.

Amongst the miscellaneous records of British envoys, agents and ambassadors are the letter books of Sir Balthasar Gerbier, minister at Brussels (1631 to 1642); correspondence of the commissioners appointed to oversee the demolition of the fortifications of Dunkirk under the terms of the Treaty of Utrecht; letter books of the Secretary of State concerning peace negotiations at Utrecht (1711 to 1714); letter books of missions involved in peace negotiations with France (1698 to 1772) and missions to the Imperial Diet and states within the Holy Roman Empire.

Also included are the collections of the corres-pondence and papers of individual diplomats, notably Sir George Stepney (1663 to 1707) con-cerning his missions to German states and the Holy Roman Empire, and Sir Joseph Williamson (1633 to 1701) and Sir Leoline Jenkins (1623 to 1685) concerning their negotiations at the congresses of Cologne (1673) and Nimeguen (1676). Correspondence of the resident minister at the court of Tuscany includes dispatches from the government agent Philip von Stosch con-cerning the movements of the Old Pretender and the Jacobite court.

Levant Company out-letter books to 1670 are described in the *Calendar of State Papers (Domestic Series)* of the reign of Charles II; these are available for consultation in the Map and Large Document Room at Kew.

POPLAR UNION.

DESERTED CHILDREN

NOTICE IS HEREBY GIVEN that, on the 12th day of December next, the Guardians of the Poor of the Poplar Union will proceed to consider the question of the expediency of assisting the

EMIGRATION TO CANADA

Of such of the following children as may be then maintained in the District or other School chargeable to this Union by reason of their having been deserted, or otherwise abandoned, by their Parents, and who by age, physical capacity and otherwise may then be found to be eligible for such emigration, namely:—

NAMES.	Ages.	NAMES.	Ages.
BYFORD, WILLIAM	11	HAGERTY, ELLEN	11
„ FREDERICK	9	HEWSON, GEORGE	11
BROWNING, SAMUEL	7	„ JOSEPH	10
„ FREDERICK	5	HODGE, EVA	8
BERRY, ALFRED	12	MAKER, GEORGE	5
„ FREDERICK	8	„ ELIZABETH	4
BRIGHTWELL, ELIZABETH	11	MEREDITH, EMMA	10
BROWN, DOLLY	12	„ „ CHARLES	8
BRIAN, JAMES	9	„ „ WALTER	7
„ MARY	6	MONK, MARY ANN	11
„ PATRICK		„ ELIZA	9
BRITTAIN, ADA	9	„ RACHEL	6
„ CHARLES	3	MARTIN, FREDERICK	8
„ WILLIAM	2	„ HENRY	7
BOLTON, BERTIE	5	„ AMELIA	4
„ EDITH	8	NEWBERRY, ALBERT	11
CAVERLEY, ARCHIBALD	10	„ WILLIAM	9
CRAWLEY, ANN MARY	13	OLDING, SUSAN	7
CALLAGHAN, MARGARET	9	OXHALL, RICHARD	5
„ ELLEN	6	„ EDWARD	3
DEELY, LOUISA	4	PRATT, ROBERT	9
ELLICK, SARAH	16	ROWBOTHAM, WILLIAM	5
„ LOUISA	14	SOUTH, CATHERINE	11
HOLMES, CHARLOTTE	12	„ GEORGE	8
„ JANE	9	SHERVILLE, PERCY	8
HAMILTON, ARTHUR JOHN	11	SHACHL, ALBERT	11
„ „ WILLIAM	7	SILK, HARRIET	10
„ „ GEORGE	4	WHITWROWE, JENNIE	4
HARVEY, RICHARD	10	WHITE, AGNES	12
„ „ GEORGE	6	„ MARGARET	4
„ „ MARGARET	2	WILLIAMS, JOHN	11
HUGHES, ALBERT	13	WARD, MARY ANN	14
„ FANNY	12	WILKINSON, THOMAS	11
HANCOCK, ALICE	12	„ „ SARAH	10
„ „ ARTHUR	10	„ „ HENRY	6
„ „ HERBERT	8	WILLMOTT, JEFFREY	10
„ „ ALBERT	3	„ „ SARAH	4
„ „ OLIVE	3		
„ „ HENRY	1		

BY ORDER,

JAMES R. COLLINS, Clerk.

Union Offices: High Street, Poplar.
September 12th, 1884.

Child migration

- The purposes and practices of child migration
- Wartime migration
- Australian child migration schemes
- Changing attitudes
- Discovering the records
  Migration of pauper children
  Child evacuation overseas
  Sources overseas

There is a long history of British child emigration schemes, which operated from 1618 to 1967. During this period some 150,000 children, many in the care of the voluntary organizations arranging their migration, were sent to British colonies and dominions – primarily America, Australia and Canada, but also Rhodesia (Zimbabwe), New Zealand, South Africa and the Caribbean. The peak period was between the 1870s and 1914: during this time child migrants to Canada alone totalled 80,000.

The purposes and practices of child migration

The aim of child migration was often to increase the population within the colonies, and to improve labour and productivity there. Although most schemes were presented as being for the benefit and the welfare of the child, few schemes actually took the feelings of the children into account.

It was estimated that in the mid-18th century, one in three of all paupers was under 16. This put an enormous strain on Poor Law authorities who could not find apprenticeships for all pauper children. The Poor Law Amendment Act 1850 (cap c. I), allowed Boards of Guardians to send children under 16 overseas for the first time (though it was not until 1870 that the majority of schemes began to take place).

Between 1869 and the early 1930s over 100,000 children were sent to Canada from Great Britain during the child emigration movement. One of the first parties of young paupers to be taken to Canada was led by the Evangelical Maria Rye. Annie Macpherson, with Maria Rye, had opened schools for destitute children in London and Liverpool in 1870 and most of her migrants came from these institutions rather than workhouse schools. Such schemes (like those carried out by other voluntary groups such as Dr Barnardo's Homes and the Canadian Catholic Emigration Committee) had to arrange for the reception of the children in Canada, and for their subsequent settlement in suitable families. In 1874, the Local Government Board (LGB) despatched an inspector to Canada to assess the conditions of emigration and welfare arrangements. The inspector, Andrew Doyle, was critical of a number of points, one of which was the high demand of physical work in the farmsteads which was being put upon children as young as seven. As a result of the Doyle report, in March 1875 the LGB withdrew its approval of pauper child emigration, though voluntary organizations

Spotlight: The legacy of child migration

Up to 1967 some 150,000 children were sent overseas to settle and grow up in Canada, Australia, New Zealand and Southern Rhodesia. Many were sent to orphanages, and charitable and religious institutions. Common-wealth governments, particularly in Australia, supported the schemes and encouraged organizations such as Barnado's, the National Children's Homes and the Fairbridge Society to continue settling children in new homes overseas. However, many child migrants later claimed that they were ill treated and suffered abuse in many of the institutions.

Child migrants are represented in the UK by a number of organizations. The Child Migrants Trust was established in 1987 to assist child migrants trying to find their 'lost' families in the UK. Child migrants and the Child Migrants Trust have lobbied for compensation and an apology from governments. Other bodies that offer assistance are, in the UK, Barnardo's Aftercare (Ilford, Essex), the Catholic Child Welfare Council and Australian Child Migrant Project (Coleshill, Birmingham). In Australia there are the International Association of Former Child Migrants and Their Families (Perth and Melbourne), the Christian Brothers Ex-Residents Services (Perth) and the Catholic Migrant Centre (Subiaco, Western Australia).

continued to send non-pauper children. In 1884, on the condition that certain welfare conditions were met, the LGB relaxed its prohibition on pauper child emigration. The sending of the children and their eventual placement remained the responsibility of the sending agencies.

During the First World War there was a temporary halt to child migration, and by 1920 mass emigration of lone pauper children to Canada had effectively ended. Over 80,000 children had migrated to the Dominion of Canada before 1918.

Schemes between 1910 and 1960 set up by the UK, South Africa, Canada, New Zealand and Australia included movements such as those managed by Dr. Barnardo's Homes, the Fairbridge Society, the Overseas Migration Board and the Big Brother emigration scheme. This last one was a voluntary organization set up in 1925 for the purpose of fostering the emigration to Australia of boys aged 16 and 17 and 'big brothering' them, in place of their families, until the age of at least 21. The Big Brother scheme attracted over 2,000 children before the Second World War and a further 1,400 between 1947 and 1954. The boys, recruited through UK press publicity and applications to orphanages, were selected to work in trades in Tasmania and New South Wales, mainly working in the agricultural industry.

Wartime migration

In May 1940 the growing menace to the UK from both invasion and mass air attack led to spontaneous offers of hospitality for British children from the Dominions and the USA. Offers were received through the Canadian government and on 31 May from private homes in Canada. In a few days similar offers were received from Australia, New Zealand, South Africa and the USA.

On 7 June 1940, the Children's Overseas Reception Board (CORB) was set up to deal with these offers. It took the form of an Inter-Departmental Committee under the Chairman-ship of Geoffrey Shakespeare MP, Parliamentary Under Secretary of State to the Dominions Office. The committee was appointed jointly by the Secretary of State for the Dominions and the Minister of Health, and was formed of represen-tatives from the Home Office, Foreign Office, Ministry of Pensions, Scottish Office, Ministry of Health, Board of Education, Ministry of Shipping, Ministry of Labour, Treasury and the Dominions Office. Its terms of reference were:

> To consider offers from overseas to house and care for children, whether accompanied or

unaccompanied, from the European war zone, residing in Great Britain, including children orphaned by the war and to make recommendations thereon.

An advisory council consisting of representatives of various societies interested in migration and youth organizations was also appointed by the chairman of the Board to advise him on the various aspects of selection, welfare and reception overseas.

A special Board for Scotland, with its own advisory council, was also set up. It followed the policy laid down by the Board in London, and a Scottish liaison officer was appointed to keep the Scottish Board informed of the daily decisions and progress.

These boards and advisory councils and their staff, with the help of local authorities, were responsible for dealing with applications, sorting, selecting and approving the children, contacting the parents, arranging parties of children for sailing, providing escorts, collecting the children at the ports and seeing them off, and also corresponding with the Dominions authorities about reception and care overseas and the eventual return of the children after the war. The boards, and their advisory councils, were disbanded in 1944 once the perceived threat from German military activity had diminished.

Prior to the setting up of CORB, some 11,000 children had been evacuated overseas via private schemes. A total of 3,100 children were sent to Australia, Canada, New Zealand and South Africa under the CORB scheme between July and September 1940. Evacuation ceased on 17 September 1940 when the vessel SS *City of Benares* was torpedoed with the loss of 77 Canada-bound children on board. All future CORB sailings were cancelled, even though the Board remained active until its disbandment four years later. Many CORB children returned to the UK after the end of hostilities to be reunited with their families.

Australian child migration schemes

Between 1947 and 1953 over 3,000 children from the UK migrated to Australia under approved child migration schemes. Other European countries were asked if they would like to participate in the child migration scheme but only the UK and Malta accepted.

Over 30 homes were approved by the Commonwealth for the housing of child migrants. Most of these were run by voluntary and religious organizations. It was not government policy to provide homes specifically for migrant children; however, the Australian government did contribute towards the capital expenditure incurred by these organizations in setting up suitable homes. Both the Commonwealth and state governments in Australia contributed towards running costs. The governments of the United Kingdom and Malta also paid maintenance for their children who had emigrated to approved institutions in Australia.

Children constituted a particularly attractive category of migrant because they were seen to assimilate more easily, were more adaptable, had a long working life ahead and could be cheaply housed in dormitory-style accommodation.

As the role of the Commonwealth government was mainly that of an overseer (the programmes being administered by the states), most of the records held by the National Archives of Australia are general policy files. Some series of child migrant case files are held by a number of Australian state archives.

The Commonwealth Department of Immigration was responsible for approving the entry of individuals and recording their arrival. Matters such as accommodation, welfare and reception arrangements generally lay with state governments or charitable bodies such as the Big Brother Movement, Dr Barnardo's Homes, Fairbridge Farm Schools or institutions run by religious orders.

Changing attitudes

For its part, the UK government has considered that such policies and schemes were misguided. As a direct result of the House of Commons 1997–8 Third Report from the Health Select Committee into the Welfare of Former Child Migrants, the British government announced in 1999 several measures to assist former British child migrants to trace their personal records and travel to the UK to reunite with close family, from whom they were separated and with whom they lost contact with when they migrated to Australia. The government has therefore set up two new kinds of help: the Child Migrant Central Information Index and the Support Fund.

The Child Migrant Central Information Index contains basic information about individual child migrants taken from the available UK records of known sending agencies. The Index acts as a signpost to the sending agencies holding personal records, and is available to former child migrants themselves, parents and siblings of child migrants and any nominated representatives. As access is restricted, the Index will not be made available over the Internet. Initially, it relates to those child migrants who were sent to Australia, Canada and New Zealand on government-assisted schemes between 1920 and the late 1960s. It will not be a complete listing of all former child migrants, and for various reasons some original records will not be available: some were destroyed during the Second World War; some agencies may no longer exist and may not have transferred their records to another repository for preservation; some records may have been lost; some agencies may not have been very clear in identifying some migrants as children; and problems may arise from poor transcripts or handwriting. Further enquiries about the Index should be made to the National Council of Voluntary Child Care Organisations.

Discovering the records

Migration of pauper children
The earliest evidence of poor children migrating overseas is in 1617 when the Virginia Company in America asked for children to be sent to their colony. The City of London then responded by

sending over 100 poor and orphaned children from Christ's Hospital School, and school registers in the custody of the Guildhall Library include the names of some 1,000 children who were sent to America.

At the National Archives, there is a range of records relating to child migration. The series of records MH 102 covers all aspects of child detention in remand homes and industrial and approved schools, including subjects such as absconding, education, general health and welfare, boarding out, fostering and adoption, holiday camps, emigration, employment and aftercare. Related policy files in the CHN (Children) series, which originated in the Home Office in 1949, can be found in BN 29 and BN 62, with representative case files in BN 28. Although the vast majority of these records are closed for 75 years, under the Freedom of Information Act 2000 it is possible to request a review of the information closed records contain. To do this, you must request a review in writing to the National Archives or follow the links at piece level on the catalogue, which will trigger a review request.

You can access earlier files in the general series of Home Office registered papers in HO 45 and HO 144. Mainly policy and correspondence files relating to the emigration of children under the Children Act 1908, ch. 67, these records include schemes for the emigration of children to Canada and Australia.

The records concerning child emigration in MH 102 are mainly policy and correspondence files relating to schemes between 1910 and 1960, such as movements set up by Dr Barnardo's Homes, the Fairbridge Society, the Overseas Migration Board and the Big Brother emigration scheme. Again, some personnel files are closed for 75 or 100 years, including MH 102/2254 which contains detailed lists of children sailing for Australia under the Fairbridge Society scheme in 1950–4.

Local Government Board Poor Law records in MH 12 tend to record only statistical information on the numbers of children sent overseas, though you can sometimes find Poor Law Union posters giving notice of the names and ages of children being sent abroad. These records are arranged by the name of the Poor Law Union.

Similarly, you may need to access MH 19: Local Government Board and Predecessors: Correspondence with Government Offices, 1834–1909. This series contains correspondence of the Poor Law Commission and Board and the Local Government Board with other government departments, the Metropolitan Police, the

Metropolitan Board of Works and parliamentary officers relating to Poor Law administration and, after 1871, public health and local government services. The series includes volumes of internal correspondence and papers of the Poor Law Board and the Local Government Board (LGB), including draft orders and Bills, minutes and memoranda on establishment and organization matters, precedents, general questions of administration and correspondence with the Treasury. Some volumes relate to specific subjects, particularly plague, but also anthrax, cholera, leprosy, smallpox, yellow fever, quarantine and emigration. The records are arranged by names of corresponding departments. Registers of correspondence are in MH 20.

There is a particularly interesting record providing an insight into child migration policy. MH 19/9 contains Local Government Board copies of enclosures and reports regarding emigration of pauper children to Canada, 1887–92. Within this document, there are detailed reports on pauper child emigrants resident in Canada between 1887 and 1892. The reports, compiled by the Secretary Department of Agriculture on instruction from the Dominion of Canada Immigration Officer, give comments about their condition, health, character, schooling and frequency of church attendance, and on each child's view of their new homes. The reports cite the Union or parish from which they were sent, as well as each child's name and age and host's name and address. Further Canadian government inspectors' reports and statistical information regarding child migrants can be found in Parliamentary Papers, available on microfiche in the Microfilm Reading Room, and online.

ARCHIVES OF VOLUNTARY AGENCIES
You may find that archives of the voluntary agencies provide more details of individual migrating children. Maria Rye's records can be found among the records of the Church of England Children's Bureau at Old Kennington Town Hall, London. Annie Macpherson's records and those relating to the work of Dr Barnardo's Homes are in the custody of the Sydney Jones Library at the University of Liverpool. These records include registers of child emigrants and case files. Such personal archives are subject to access restrictions, usually remaining closed for 100 years. In addition to these archives, Barnardo's retains an extensive archive of some 400,000 photographs, dating from 1866 onwards, detailing the work of the charity. Many other records of child migration to Canada, including

some of Dr Barnardo's archives, may now be found at the National Archives of Canada.

Child evacuation overseas
At the National Archives, the series DO 131 relates to the records of the Children's Overseas Records Board (CORB) records and the 3,100 children sent to Australia, Canada, New Zealand and South Africa between July and September 1940. You will find that these records are quite detailed. They consist of administrative files, a selection of case files relating to children (DO 131/94–105), their escorts (DO 131/71–87) and registers of child applicants (DO 131/106–113), though the majority of these files were destroyed under statute in 1959. Dominions Office policy files relating to the activities of the Board are in DO 35.

Migrating children are included in the series of records BT 27: Outwards Passenger Lists for the period 1890–1960. Information from these records includes name of child, age, address in UK and country of origin. The records are arranged chronologically and by UK port of departure, though there are plans to digitize this series and make it available online with a personal name index (*see* Chapter 6 for more information).

Sources overseas

Records relating to child migrants to Australia – including migrant selection documents, passenger lists and immigration policy files – are held by the various state archives, such as the National Archives in Sydney, the National Archives in Canberra and the Melbourne Archives Centre. Check the website of the National Archives of Australia for further information.

You will find that the range of papers usually found in the files identified as migrant selection documents includes application forms, medical reports and other papers completed by applicants for assisted migration to Australia from Britain. Consolidated, they contain a wide range of personal details. From November 1948, papers were arranged chronologically by arrival date of the vessel or aircraft. For example, personal documents of British migrants and British assisted passage migrants, which include children, are held from 1947 to 1968 in collections at the National Archives in Sydney.

Passenger records, which include passenger lists and passenger cards, provide a rich source of family history information. Each vessel arriving at the Australian ports was required to lodge a list of incoming passengers. Arranged by date and port of arrival, passenger lists include the name of each passenger and, in earlier lists, details such as age or marital status. There are no name indexes to these records so, unless date and port of arrival is known, a search is likely to be time-consuming with no guarantee of success. Passenger lists survive for all Australian ports from 1924, with some gaps. Passenger lists will often need to be consulted to establish the ship's name and date of arrival needed to access the migrant selection documents.

Files referring to child migration will be found in the main correspondence series of the Department of Immigration in Sydney, and some will contain information about individual children. Records are often arranged by the name of the sending agency, such as Dr Barnardo's Homes.

Relevant records on child migration may also be held by the state government archives in Australia. The Child Migrants' Trust can assist in tracing the background and families of children who came to Australia as unaccompanied child migrants. In addition, the Western Australia Former Child Migrants Referral Index contains basic information about child migrants to Australia between 1913 and 1968.

If your interest relates to child migration to Canada you should check the website of the Library and Archives Canada. Over 100,000 children were sent to Canada from Great Britain between 1869 and the early 1930s. Members of the British Isles Family History Society of Greater Ottawa are locating and indexing the names of these 'Home Children' found in passenger lists in the custody of the National Archives of Canada, and the database is searchable via the National Archives of Canada website.

Chapter 11

Matters of life and death

- At home
- At sea
- Overseas
- Discovering the records
  Statutory registration
  Ecclesiastical records
  Foreign congregations in England
  Marine and Board of Trade records
  Overseas records
  Armed forces returns

If you are tracing your immigrant ancestors to Britain, you may need to consult the birth, marriage and death records of their descendants within the country for clues. Alternatively, if pursuing your emigrant ancestors your focus may well be on the records of those who were born, married or died abroad or even in transit.

At home

The births, baptisms, marriages, deaths and burials of people living in the United Kingdom will in most cases be found in the usual religious and statutory registration records. Parish registers and nonconformist registers for those who joined the Church of England or Protestant churches or chapels will be held locally in county record offices. The National Archives at Kew holds some nonconformist records and a very few Roman Catholic records. Most Roman Catholic registers and synagogue records both before and after civil registration should be consulted locally and through the relevant religious authorities.

From 1837 for England and Wales, from 1855 for Scotland, and 1864 for Ireland, all births, marriages and deaths will be recorded in local register offices and centrally at the General Register Offices in London, Edinburgh and Dublin (also Belfast for Northern Ireland from 1922). Army chaplains made returns of soldiers' marriages and the births and deaths of soldiers' families. Regimental registers and chaplains' returns record army events at home from 1761 and abroad from c.1790. After 1837, it is sometimes possible to find a civil birth certificate and an entry in the army records if the event occurred in this country.

At sea

Births, marriages and deaths at sea may be recorded in the log of the ship concerned. From 1837 English births and deaths at sea were recorded by masters of merchant vessels and captains of Royal Naval vessels and forwarded to the General Register Office in London. Returns were made to the Board of Trade from 1854 and the information forwarded to the General Register Office. Scottish births and deaths at sea are held by the General Register Office in Edinburgh from 1855. Irish births and deaths at sea are held by the General Register Office in Dublin from 1864. Depending on where the individual was resident in the UK, the relevant General Register Office would have been informed.

Spotlight: Oscar Wilde and Ramsay MacDonald

Many famous Brits were born, married, or died overseas or at sea, and their records can be found at the National Archives.

Following his spell in Reading Gaol, after being convicted of then-illegal homosexual practices, the poet-playwright and wit Oscar Wilde took himself into exile in France. He died in Paris, on 30 November 1900, and was buried at Bagneux two days later, though his remains were transferred to the much grander Père Lachaise cemetery in 1919. His death is recorded in the document RG 35/35, page 1077.

On 9 November 1937 the former prime minister Ramsay MacDonald died of heart failure, following a game of deck quoits on the liner *Reina del Pacifico*, bound for South America. His body was returned to Britain on the naval cruiser HMS *Apollo*. His death is recorded in the document BT 334/94.

Overseas

Ecclesiastical records in former British colonies will usually remain in those countries. Some records or more usually copies of registers – transcripts – were returned to London to the Bishop of London's Registry, the Bishop of

London having an overseas jurisdiction before colonial dioceses began to be created from the mid-19th century onwards. The Bishop of London retained responsibility for churches in southern Europe until 1842 when the diocese of Gibraltar was created, and northern and central Europe until 1980. Jurisdiction ceased in the American states after 1776, but remained in most British colonies until the 19th century. Records of churches and chapels in India were returned but found their way to the India Office in London.

Statutory registration of births, marriages and deaths of English residents occurring in foreign countries did not begin until 1849. Since then returns from British consuls have been made to the Registrar General in London. The General Register Office, Edinburgh, holds Scottish births and deaths overseas and marriages overseas from 1860. Irish births and deaths abroad from 1864 were registered at the General Register Office in Dublin.

Records of military units abroad and on ships at sea were recorded by military chaplains and returned to the General Register Office in London. Royal Navy deaths are recorded in the Marine Register. RAF registrations commence in 1920, and registrations on civil aircraft from 1947.

Civil or statutory registration began in different colonies at different periods. These records will have remained in the countries themselves and you will need to contact the authorities in each country.

Discovering the records

Statutory registration

The Family Records Centre holds the indexes to births, marriages and deaths registered in England and Wales. The actual records of births, marriages and deaths for England and Wales are held by the General Register Office (Office for National Statistics). You can order certificates by telephone, post or email if you have the references; year, quarter, registration district, volume and page number from the indexes.

Scottish registration indexes for births from 1855 to 1905, marriages from 1855 to 1930 and deaths from 1855 to 1955 can be searched online at the Scotland's People website on a pay per view basis. For records of registration in Ireland and Northern Ireland (after 1922) there are no online indexes. The records are held in the General Register Offices in Dublin and Belfast.

Ecclesiastical records
Parish registers of the Church of England are now mainly deposited in local and county record offices. Registers for parishes in Scotland, from about 1553 to 1854, are held by the General Register Office for Scotland, and indexes to the registers are available on the Scotland's People website. Information on the registers of the Church of Ireland, many of which were lost in 1922, can be found on the websites of the National Archives of Ireland and the Public Record Office of Northern Ireland.

The Society of Genealogists holds copies of most published or transcribed parish registers of England and Wales. The Society also has copies of some overseas registers and indexes to others.

Foreign congregations in England
RG 4: Registers of Births, Marriages and Deaths surrendered to the Non-parochial Registers Commissions of 1837 and 1857 includes registers of the Walloon and French Protestant churches in England and also registers of the Dutch, German and French Chapels Royal at St James's Palace. These records are available on microfilm at the Family Records Centre and at the National Archives, Kew.

The London Metropolitan Archives holds the records of the German Hamburg Lutheran Church (LMA ref: ACC/2622) and of some other German churches (*see* LMA Information Leaflet No. 17, *The German Community in London*). The Anglo-German Family History Society has produced microfiche indexes to St George's German Lutheran Church records (copies available at the Family Records Centre and the London Metropolitan Archives).

Marine and Board of Trade records
Births and deaths at sea can be searched for in the Marine Registers. The indexes are available at the Family Records Centre and microfiche copies are available at the National Archives, Kew. Board of Trade registers are held by the National Archives. Following the Merchant Shipping Act 1854, registers of births, marriages and deaths are recorded using information from ships' official logs in the series BT 158. Births, marriages and deaths are recorded from 1854 to 1883, just births and deaths from 1883 to 1887, and deaths only from 1888 to 1890. There is also a register of births of British nationals at sea from 1875 to 1891 in BT 160, and deaths of British nationals at sea from 1875 to 1888 in BT 159. Registers of births, marriages

and deaths at sea from 1891 to 1972 are in BT 334.

The Guildhall Library has some records of baptisms and burials at sea from 1894 to 1952 (ref. Ms 11827) and baptisms at sea from 1955 to 1961 (Ms 11817 and index in Ms 15061/1–2, under 'Sea'). Other baptisms are in the international memoranda at the Guildhall Library.

Overseas records
The Bishop of London's archives of registers and transcripts are held at the Guildhall Library, and a few registers can be found in the National Archives and Lambeth Palace Library. The International Memoranda cover various dates, the earliest 1788, the latest 1924, and are held in the Guildhall Library; they contain baptisms, marriages and burials from overseas made by chaplains officiating in British embassies and legations abroad, and also clergymen resident or travelling abroad or on board ships (Ms 10926/1–13). The Bishop of Gibraltar's memoranda covers miscellaneous baptisms from 1921 to 1969, including many from clergy on board ships (Ms 23607).

India Office registers can now be found in the British Library Asia, Pacific and African Collections.

The General Register Office, Office for National Statistics, keeps all the statutory returns with indexes available at the Family Records Centre and microfiche copies are held in the Microfilm Reading Room at the National Archives. Some original registers from which the statutory returns were made have been deposited in the National Archives by the Foreign Office and can be found in various FO series. The General Register Office indexes at the Family Records Centre and the National Archives can be used to find entries in these registers.

In addition to these records, there are also non-statutory returns deposited originally by the Bishop of London with the Registrar General and now in the National Archives in five RG series: Miscellaneous Foreign Returns RG 32 from 1831 to 1969, Foreign Registers and Returns RG 33 covering various dates from 1627 to 1960, Miscellaneous Foreign Marriages RG 34 from 1826 to 1921, Miscellaneous Foreign Deaths RG 35 from 1830 to 1921, and Registers and Returns of Births, Marriages and Death in Protectorates, etc., in RG 36 covering various dates from 1895 to 1965. Indexes to all these series are in RG 43, and are available on microfilm at the Family Records Centre and the National Archives.

Armed forces returns

Military returns of births, marriages and deaths at home and abroad, and at sea, can be found in the Regimental Registers (1761–1924) and the Chaplains' Returns (1796–1880) held by the General Register Office. The indexes are at the Family Records Centre and microfiche copies are available at the National Archives, Kew. A few baptisms (1939–47) and banns (1944–7) of Palestine forces are in TNA series WO 156/6–8. A few records are held at the Guildhall Library: baptisms, marriages and burials for the Cape of Good Hope garrison from 1795 to 1803 (ref. Ms 11569), and for the Gibraltar garrison from 1807 to 1812 (Ms 10446D); British Army of the Rhine civilian baptisms from 1949 to 1961 and 1969 to 1976 (Ms 11225–5B).

Navy birth, baptism, marriage and burial records of the Chaplain of the Fleet and the Naval Chaplaincy Service can be found in TNA series ADM 338 covering various stations, barracks and dockyards at home and abroad (1845–1998).

Army and other services registrations form one series (1881–1955). There is another series for service departments (1956–65) and one for civilians and armed forces from 1966. The Family Records Centre holds indexes (microfiche copies at Kew), and many can be accessed online.

Useful addresses

The following list includes a selection of principal information sources in the UK. The National Archive's free online Archon directory (*www.nationalarchives.gov.uk/archon/*) contains a comprehensive listing. The foreign archives (*www.nationalarchives.gov.uk/archon/foreign.htm*) gives information for many institutions abroad.

Baptist Missionary Society, Regent's Park College, Pusey St, Oxford OX1 2LB Tel: 01865 288142, *www.rpc.ox.ac.uk/rpc*

Barnardo's Photographic and Film Archive, Tanners Lane, Barkingside, Ilford, Essex IG6 1QL

Borthwick Institute for Archives, University of York, York YO10 5DD, Tel: 01904 642315, *www.york.ac.uk/inst/bihr/*

British Library, 96 Euston Road, London NW1 2DB, Tel: 020 7412 7332, *www.bl.uk*

British Library Newspaper Collection, Colindale Avenue, London NW9 5HE, Tel: 020 7412 7353, *www.bl.uk/collections/newspapers.html*

Child Migrants Trust-UK, 28A Musters Road, West Bridgford, Nottingham, NG2 7PL, Tel: 0115 982 2811

Church Mission Society, Partnership House, 157 Waterloo Road, London SE1 8UU, Tel: 020 7928 8681, *www.cms-uk.org*

Corporation of London Record Office, *see* London Metropolitan Archives

Family Records Centre, 1 Myddelton Street, London EC1R 1UW, Tel: (general enquiries about certificates) 0845 603 7788, (other enquiries) 020 8392 5300, *www.familyrecords.gov.uk/frc/*

Guildhall Library, Aldermanbury, London EC2P 2EJ, Tel: 020 7332 1868/1870, *www.cityoflondon.gov.uk/corporation/leisure_heritage/*

Hartley Library, University of Southampton, Highfield, Southampton SO17 1BJ, Tel: 0238 059 2180, *www.soton.ac.uk/library*

Home Office, Departmental Record Officer, Record Management Services, 50 Queen Anne's Gate, London SW1H 9AT, *www.homeoffice.gov.uk*

Home Office Immigration and Nationality Directorate,
Reliance House, 20 Water Street, Liverpool L2 8XU,
www.ind.homeoffice.gov.uk

Huguenot Library, University College London, London WC1E
6BT, Tel: 020 7679 5199, *www.ucl.ac.uk/Library/huguenot*

Lambeth Palace Library, London SE1 7JU, Tel: 020 7928 6222,
www.lambethpalacelibrary.org

London Metropolitan Archives, 40 Northampton Road,
London EC1R OAB, *www.cityoflondon.gov.uk/lma*

Manchester Local Studies Unit, Central Library, St Peter's
Square, Manchester, M2 5PD, Tel: 0161 234 1980,
www.manchester.gov.uk/libraries/arls/

Manx Heritage Library, Manx Museum, Douglas, Isle of Man
IM1 3LY, Tel: 01624 648000, *www.gov.im/mnh/*

Merseyside Maritime Museum Library and Archives, Albert
Dock, Liverpool, L3 4AQ, Tel: 0151 478 4499,
www.liverpoolmuseums.org.uk/maritime/

The National Archives, Kew, Richmond, Surrey, TW9 4DU, Tel:
020 8876 3444, *www.nationalarchives.gov.uk*

National Archives of Scotland, HM General Register House,
Edinburgh, EH1 3YY, Tel: 0131 535 1314, *www.nas.gov.uk*

National Children's Bureau, 8 Wakeley Street, London EC1V
7QE, Tel: 020 7843 6000, *www.ncb.org.uk*

National Council of Voluntary Child Care Organisations, Unit
4, Pride Court, 80–82 White Lion Street, London N1 9PF,
Tel: 020 7713 5937, *www.ncvcco.org*

National Maritime Museum, Maritime Information Centre,
Romney Road, London SE10 9NF, Tel: 020 8858 4422,
www.nmm.ac.uk

School of Oriental and African Studies, Thornhaugh Street,
London WC1H OXG, Tel: 020 7898 4180, *www.soas.ac.uk*

Society of Genealogists, 14 Charterhouse Buildings, Goswell
Road, London EN1M 7BA, Tel: 020 7251 8799,
www.sog.org.uk

Sydney Jones Library, Chatham Street, Liverpool L69 3DA,
Tel: 0151-794-2679, *www.liv.ac.uk/Library/info/libinf_sjl.html*

University of Birmingham, Edgbaston, Birmingham B15 2TT,
www.bham.ac.uk/

Useful websites

See also the institutional websites listed under 'Useful addresses'.

Sources in the UK

www.a2a.org.uk The Access to Archives database.

www.art-science.com/agfhs/ Anglo-German Family History Society.

www.britishorigins.com Pay-per-view site offering access to a wide range of records.

www.casbah.ac.uk The Caribbean Studies Black and Asian History Archives.

www.englishorigins.com see *www.britishorigins.com*.

www.familysearch.org Family history site of the Church of Jesus Christ of Latter-day Saints, including the International Genealogical Index (IGI).

www.fco.gov.uk/travel The Foreign and Commonwealth Office.

www.gro.gov.uk The General Register Office (Office for National Statistics).

www.llgc.org.uk The National Library of Wales.

www.movinghere.org.uk For a wealth of information on immigrants to the UK.

www.nationalarchives.gov.uk/catalogue The National Archives online catalogue.

www.nationalarchives.gov.uk/census/ For censuses online.

www.nationalarchives.gov.uk/documentsonline/wills.asp For wills online.

www.nationalarchives.gov.uk/nra/ The National Register of Archives.

www.oldbaileyonline.org Old Bailey.

www.proni.gov.uk/records/church.htm Public Record Office of Northern Ireland.

www.rootsweb.com/~ukaifhg/ Anglo-Italian Family History Society.

www.sca.lib.liv.ac.uk/collections/ Gypsy and traveller collections at the Sydney Jones Library, University of Liverpool.

www.scotlandspeople.gov.uk Access to births, marriages and
   deaths indexes, census returns and parish registers for
   Scotland.
www.sog.org.uk The Society of Genealogists.

Some archives and libraries abroad

www.archives.ca Library and Archives Canada.
www.archives.gov US National Archives.
http://archives.govt.nz/ Archives New Zealand.
www.gov.mb.ca/chc/archives/hbca/ Hudson's Bay Company
   Archives.
www.gsv.org.au Genealogical Society of Victoria.
www.naa.gov.au National Archives of Australia.
www.national.archives.gov.za National Archives of South Africa.
www.nationalarchives.ie/genealogy/church.html Registers of
   the Church of Ireland.

Sources for departure records

http://home.att.net/~arnielang/shipgide.html Immigration and
   ships' passenger lists to the USA.
http://home.att.net/~wee-monster/ei.html Ships' passenger
   lists to the New World.
http://home.att.net/~wee-monster/onlinelists.html Internet
   sources for transcribed passenger records and
   indexes.
http://members.iinet.net.au/~reginald/convicts.htm#references
   Full lists of convicts transported to Western Australia
   between 1850 and 1887, giving details of offences.
www.ancestry.co.uk For locating ships' passenger lists for Irish
   immigrants into the port of New York, 1846–51.
www.beavis.co.uk/pslist.htm For 50,000 names and details
   from some Board of Trade passenger lists for Australia-
   bound vessels for the years 1909–14.
www.blaxland.com/ozships/ Includes selected Australian
   arrivals and departures, 1788–1968.
www.collectionscanada.ca/archivianet/02011802_e.html For
   migrants to Canada between 1925 and 1935.

www.ellisisland.org For over 22 million passengers and members of the ship's crews who came through Ellis Island and the port of New York between 1892 and 1924.

www.linktoyourroots.hamburg.de/ If you think your ancestors emigrated from Europe to the New World via Hamburg, 1854–1930.

www.nationalarchives.ie/topics/transportation/search01.html For records of convicts transported from Ireland between 1769 and 1853.

www.rootsweb.com Includes names of passengers from a multitude of ports from 1500s to 1900s.

www.theshipslist.com For ships' passenger lists to the New World.

Two sources for Africa, Asia and South America

http://members.ozemail.com.au/~clday For people tracing their British, European and Anglo-Indian family history in India, Burma, Pakistan and Bangladesh.

www.sun.ac.za/gisa/bronne.htm For South African genealogy.

Sources for migrant children

www.collectionscanada.ca/archivianet/020110_e.html National Archives of Canada Home Children index.

http://freepages.genealogy.rootsweb.com/~britishhomechildren Essential site for researching the British Home Children who were sent to Canada between 1870 and 1940.

Index